The Goo~~~~~~gun in the Day of Grace Performed Until the Day of Christ

with

Christ the Best Husband
An Invitation to Young Women Unto Christ

and

The Best Gift
God's Call Upon Young Men for Their Hearts

by
Thomas Vincent
Minister of Magdalene, Milk Street, London

Edited by Rev. Don Kistler

Soli Deo Gloria Publications
. . . for instruction in righteousness . . .

Soli Deo Gloria Publications
P.O. Box 451, Morgan, PA 15064
(412) 221-1901/FAX 221-1902

*

*

ISBN 1-57358-082-1

Contents

The Good Work Begun

Contents v

The Good Work Begun

"Being confident of this very thing, that He which hath begun a good work in you will perform it until the day of Jesus Christ." Philippians 1:6

Introduction

Among all the works of men, some of which have been great and illustrious, none are comparable unto the works of God. And among all the works of God before us, none are more admirable than the work of God within us. You have sometimes seen rare and curious works of art—beautiful pictures, stately edifices and buildings. You see daily more curious works of nature, the substance of those shadows, the stately structure of the earth and heavens; but the work of grace, which cannot be seen with the eye, excels every visible work in luster and curiosity.

David tells us in Psalm 139:14–15 that his body was wonderfully made and all his members curiously wrought and fashioned by the hand of God. His soul was more wonderfully made and there was more curiosity in the forming of his spirit with faculties of such excellent use and operations. But in the new forming of the soul after the image of God, in God's drawing the linaments of the new man upon the heart, is the greatest wonder and curiosity. This is the good work which God begins and will perform. All God's works are good, but this work is excellent;

1

other works are really good, but this one is eminently good; in other works God puts forth His power and manifests His wisdom, but in this work He has shown the exceeding greatness of His power, His most admirable wisdom, and, withal, the exceeding riches of His grace and love. Other works shall be demolished—not only earthly bodies, but heavenly bodies themselves shall melt and be dissolved at last; but this good work of grace shall abide unto the day of Christ and in the day of Christ, and then be perfected in glory. Of this the Apostle expresses his confidence in the text: "Being confident of this very thing, that He which hath begun a good work in you will perform it until the day of Jesus Christ."

This epistle was written to the Philippians when the Apostle was in bonds at Rome for the testimony of the gospel. Nevertheless, the Word of God was not bound, but had a freer course and more powerful efficacy. His bonds tended to the furtherance of the gospel. The body of the Apostle was in bonds, but his heart was not in bonds, unless it was in the bonds of love for the Philippians. His tongue was not in bonds, for he let them know what prayers he offered unto God on their behalf. His pen was not in bonds, for in prison he wrote this excellent epistle to them. And we have reason to bless God for those bonds which were the occasion of a work so beneficial to the Church in all later ages.

After the Apostle's salutation to the Philippians, he administers matter of great joy and comfort to them in this text: "Being confident of this very thing, that He which hath begun a good work in you will perform it until the day of Jesus Christ." In these words we have:

1. The Apostle's confidence concerning the saints at Philippi, and, in them, of all saints unto the end of the world "Being confident of this very thing." He does not speak of it as an uncertain thing, something that might or might not be, but as of a thing most sure, a thing of which he had full confidence and persuasion.

2. Here's the thing of which he is confident, or the matter of his confidence concerning them: "That He which hath begun a good work in you will perform it until the day of Jesus Christ." Here we have the work of grace set forth by the quality of it (it is "a good work"), by the subject of it (the soul: not a work outside you, but within you), by the Author of it ("He," that is, God), by the beginning of it ("He that hath begun a good work in you"), by the accomplishment of it and bringing it to perfection ("will perform it until the day of Jesus Christ").

Hence observe these two doctrines, which I will expound upon in the following chapters:

DOCTRINE 1: The good work of grace in the soul is begun by the Lord.

DOCTRINE 2: The good work which God begins in the day of grace, He will perform until the day of Christ.

Section 1

*The first doctrine: the good work of grace
in the soul is begun by the Lord*

I n handling this point, I shall speak concerning the good work of grace itself, concerning the subject of it (which is the soul),
concerning the Author of it (and show that
it is the Lord who begins this good work), why the
Lord begins this good work, and then make some
application.

1. Concerning the good work of grace itself.
There are many evil works of men, such as are all
sins. The work of grace is the good work of God.
There are some good works which are wrought by
us; this is the good work which is wrought in us.
There are some works of grace, and gracious acts of
God towards us, which effect only a relative change,
such as God's justification of our persons, His adoption of us and admitting us into His family, but this
is a gracious work of God upon us whereby He effects within us a real change; and although the
grace within us is always accompanied with the
grace outside us, yet it is really distinct from it. This
good work of grace is begun in regeneration, or the
new birth, when God effectually calls us by His Word
and Spirit, and powerfully turns us from darkness to
light, and from the reign of sin into the subjection
and obedience of Christ. It is carried on in the work

of sanctification wherein sin, which in the first work of grace is dethroned and mortally wounded, is more and more mortified, the spiritual life first begun is maintained, and the soul is more and more quickened and enabled to live unto righteousness.

In the first work, the seed of grace is planted in the soul by the Spirit, which in the work of sanctification springs up and brings forth the fruit of holiness and obedience. In the first work of grace, all the linaments and members of the new man are formed in the soul, which in sanctification are more and more shaped and fashioned after God's image, and the new man grows up from its infancy more and more towards the stature and strength of a perfect man in Christ. In the first work, all the habits of grace are infused together into the soul, which in the work of sanctification gather strength and show themselves in their lively and vigorous exercise.

I am now to speak of the first work of grace, or the good work as it is begun by the Lord. When the Lord effects a gracious change in the soul, He finds the sinner empty and void of all good, filled with the guilt and smeared with the defilement of sin, and, notwithstanding the wounds which sin makes in his conscience, He finds him insensible. And though his danger is of everlasting ruin, He finds him asleep and secure.

First, the Lord meets with him and puts a stop to his course and career of sin, hedges up his way, as it were, with thorns. By His providence He brings the sinner under the preaching of the Word, and there He shows him the evil work and transgressions wherein he has exceeded and exceedingly provoked wherein he has exceeded and exceedingly provoked His holy eye against him. The Lord in His Word sounds His trumpet of judgment and awakens him out of his carnal security by the loud thunderings and dreadful lightnings of the law. He convinces the sinner of the guilt and desert of sin, and the danger which he is in of the eternal damnation and destruction of hell, which such impenitent and unbelieving sinners as he is are liable unto. Hereupon conscience, which before had been lulled to sleep by the devil and deceitful lusts, begins to be startled and takes up its whip to lash and its sword to prick and sensibly to wound the sinner, so that in distress he cries out, "Oh, what shall I do to be saved?"

God at first sends His Spirit (in order to the preparation of the soul for this gracious change) to be a spirit of bondage to awaken the sinner unto fear (Romans 8:15). The Spirit does, as it were, bring a warrant from heaven, and like a sergeant slaps the sinner on the back and arrests him for all his affronts and indignities which he has offered unto the King of heaven, for all the treasons and rebellions which he has practiced. The sinner, having nothing to plead, is unable to make his escape, for where could he fly from God's Spirit? This spirit of bondage lays him up in prison, as it were, puts chains and shackles upon his feet, and then passes the sentence of the law upon him: "You must die!" It lets him know that he is cursed (Galatians 3:10), condemned already (John 3:18), and that the execution is not far off.

Thus the sinner is brought into great distress and perplexity of mind. He looks about him for help, but all succor fails him. He struggles and would fain break the bonds which are upon him, but he finds himself the more entangled. He endeavors to divert his grief and throw away his troubles, but he is the more perplexed and wounded. Then he seeks after something to appease God's anger and quiet the clamors of his conscience. So he flies to duties and to ordinances; he prays and hears and reads, and turns from his former ungodly company and practices, and frequents the company of the saints and servants of God, joining with them in all religious observances and exercises. But still he finds (if God works on him effectually) that none of these can remove the guilt of one sin, and that his righteousness is at best imperfect, which results from the strictest performance of any duties. And therefore he looks upon himself as worthless and helpless in himself, and perceives that it does not lie in the power of any creature to help him.

But, having a discovery made of the Lord Jesus Christ, who is mighty and able to save to the uttermost all those who come to God by Him (Hebrews 7:25), being made acquainted with the perfect righteousness of Christ and the full satisfaction which by His death He has given unto God's justice for man's sin, and having a free offer made of this to him, and a gracious invitation to come unto Christ that he might have pardon and life by Him, being powerfully drawn by the Spirit, he is inclined and enabled to come to Him and lay hold on Him, whereby he is joined to Christ and receives life from Him. Thus the good work of grace is begun, the nature of which will appear in the second particular.

Section 2

Concerning the subject of this
good work of grace: the soul

The good work begun in you, that is, in your souls, the whole soul is the subject of this grace which the Lord works. The subject of this good work of grace is the soul, and that is the concern of this second particular.

1. In the good work of grace the understanding is enlightened and the spirit of the mind is renewed (Ephesians 4:23). The understandings of graceless persons are darkened (Ephesians 4:18). They cannot know the things of the Spirit of God because they are spiritually discerned (1 Corinthians 2:14). There is a black night upon their spirits; a darkness worse than an Egyptian night overspreads the face of their souls. There is a veil of ignorance and unbelief over their eyes, which keeps the light of the knowledge of God from them. Hence it is that they do not apprehend the beauty and excellency which is in God and Christ, and the ways of holiness.

But where God begins the good work of grace in any, He opens their eyes (Acts 26:18). He illuminates their understandings (Hebrews 10:32). He causes the darkness to pass away and the true light to shine into them (1 John 2:8). By this light He reveals to them the odious nature of sin, His own infinite excellencies and perfections, and the excellency of the ways of holiness, which lead unto life and happiness, beyond the ways of sin, which lead to death and ruin.

They had some knowledge of these things before by the teachings of men, but it was a bare, speculative, notional knowledge which they had in their heads; but now they are taught by the Spirit and attain to a spiritual, practical, experimental and heart-affecting knowledge of these things. Now they perceive a marvelous excellency in those things which before seemed foolishness to them (1 Corinthians 2:14). They have a new eye, being anointed with the spiritual eyesalve, and all things now appear with a new face. Before, sin, with its paint and bait, appeared beautiful and desirable; and Christ, with His cross and yoke, seemed an enemy rather than a friend. They could not discern His form or comeliness, and therefore they undervalued and neglected Him. But now they have a discovery of the hook through the bait, and a discovery of the ugliness through the paint of sin. It now appears most dangerous and odious to them, and they have a discovery of the loveliness of Christ's face and the ease of His yoke. He appears to them now as most precious and desirable.

Now they behold wonderful things in the law which they never before apprehended. In that glass they have a view given to them of the monstrous nature of sin, of the pollutions which it has brought upon their souls. Now they have a prospect of hell and the dreadful miseries which are the issue and product of sin.

And they also behold wonderful and glorious

things in the glass of the gospel. There they have a discovery of the great and wonderful salvation which Christ has purchased for them, of the riches and freeness of God's love unto them, of that glorious inheritance in heaven which the Lord has promised and prepared for them. They see things now in another manner than they ever did before, so that they wonder at their own former blindness and sottishness, and at other men's present folly and madness, that they should set their hearts upon the toys and trifles of the world, that they should wallow like swine in the mire of sin, and drudge on contentedly and securely in Satan's chains towards hell. In the meantime, they neglect God and Christ and their salvation, trampling under foot those inestimable riches and treasures which in the gospel are offered so freely unto them.

2. In the good work of grace, the will is rectified and put in order. The will is the great springwheel, as it were, of the soul which, while it is out of course, all the other inferior faculties, like so many little wheels depending upon it, must be disordered and distempered in their motions. But once the will is rectified, then the whole soul is brought into frame. The will is the Queen-Regent which bears great sway, and in graceless persons is exceedingly corrupt and depraved, and employs all the powers that are under her for the fulfilling and satisfaction of her base and filthy lusts. The thoughts, the fancy, the memory, the inferior affections of the soul, and the senses and members of the body are at the beck of the will to be employed in the service and as the instruments of sin. When the will is changed, the

work of grace is effected, and not before. When this fortress is taken, then Christ enters and takes possession.

In the work of grace there is a change in the will in regard to its inclination and complacency. Gracious persons have new inclinations. They like now what before they disliked, not only by a bare approbation of their understandings, but also by a complacency of their wills in it. They dislike and disrelish what before they liked and delighted themselves in, not only because of the checks and upbraiding of their consciences, but through an aversion of their wills unto it. The world appears to the understandings to be vain and empty, sin to be most odious and ugly, Christ to be most beautiful and lovely, the grace of God here and the enjoyment of Him hereafter to be their chief felicity; so the inclinations of their wills are accordingly carried forth towards these objects.

Their wills dislike the world for their portion and chief good, and therefore renounce it upon that account. They dislike sin not only because of the punishment threatened unto it, but also because of the innate filthiness which is in it. Their wills like Christ not only as a Savior to deliver them from hell, but also to deliver them from their sin. They like His blood to purify their hearts as well as to pacify God's anger and their own consciences. They like His person and beauty as well as His portion and benefits. They like Him not only with His crown, but also with His cross—with poverty, disgrace, and shame here as well as with treasures and glory in the next world. They like God's favor beyond the favor of

men or life itself. And according to their
inclination, so is their end or design, namely the
glory of God here and the enjoyment of God forever.
This sways them chiefly, and is the design which
they are carrying on in the world. Therefore their
wills make choice of suitable means, even such as
the Word reveals and directs for the attaining of this
end; accordingly also are the purposes and reso-
lutions of their wills suitable unto their end and
choice for avoiding hindrances and making use of
furtherances.

3. In the work of grace the fancy is renewed,
though not in whole, yet in part. Much of the frothi-
ness and vanity thereof is hereby corrected. It is
more ready to receive impressions of good; it is
more useful unto the sanctified mind, and more
readily subservient unto the sanctified will than it
was before.

4. In the good work of grace the conscience also
is renewed. It is awakened at first to prepare the soul
for this work, and it is afterwards kept awake and
tender so as to check and keep from sin. "How can I
do this wickedness and sin against God? How can I
spill again the blood of my Savior, or grieve and
drive away my Comforter?"

5. In the good work of grace, the memory is renewed, though not strengthened beyond its natural
capacity, in keeping and recollecting things com-
mitted to it. Yet in the work of grace it is in some
measure sanctified and cleansed from that mud and
filth of the world, and the vanity which like a sieve it
retained before, and is now made chiefly a treasury
of heavenly things.

6. In the good work of grace, the affections are renewed, the love and hatred, the desire and flight, the grief and delight, the hope and fear, and the anger—all the liking affections follow the inclination of the will and are carried forth towards God and Christ, and holiness here and happiness hereafter. The disliking affections are carried forth towards that which is offensive unto God and destructive to the soul. Thus we have dealt briefly concerning the subject of the good work of grace, and the several faculties renewed and changed in this gracious change.

Section 3

Concerning God, the Author of this good work

Grace does not grow in the garden of nature, there being no seed of it to be found therein. It is neither a natural power, such as that of the understanding, will, conscience, memory, or affections, which are to be found in all the children of Adam by nature; neither is it connatural, such as original righteousness was in Adam before his fall; neither is it a habit acquired by the multiplicity of acts, whereof there are some dispositions in nature, such as the habits of arts and sciences, and moral virtues.

Grace is a pure stream which cannot spring forth from the polluted fountain of nature. Job 14:4: "Who can bring a clean thing out of an unclean?" You never saw figs grow upon thorns or grapes upon thistles. The souls of all the fallen children of men, being wholly corrupt and depraved with original sin, it is impossible that this good should be effected by the power of nature. Some, by the strength of natural power, cultivated by education and learning, may attain much knowledge in the mysteries of nature, and by studying the Scriptures they may attain a notional knowledge of divine mysteries; but the excellency of these mysteries is hidden from them. They still remain without the spiritual discerning of the things of the Spirit without the teachings of the Spirit (1 Corinthians 2:14).

Natural men may, through observance and diligence, attain a great accomplishment as to many moral virtues, and hereby shine with some kind of luster in darker parts of the world; but by no natural power or industry can they attain unto any truly sanctifying and saving grace. The stream cannot be raised up to a greater height than the spring lies from whence it arises. And that which is natural cannot by any natural power be elevated unto that which is supernatural.

It is not from any innate power in the Word and ordinances to effect this good work of grace in the soul of any. Indeed, the Word is an instrument, and the ordinances are means of grace; but they are only instruments and means which have no virtue and efficacy in themselves unless they receive it immediately from God, the efficient cause of this work. They are but channels, not the fountain of grace. The Word is a sword, but God's hand must draw it forth and strike with it that it may wound. There was no virtue in the waters to heal (John 5) unless the angel troubled them; and there is no virtue in ordinances to change and sanctify the soul unless the Spirit moves in them and works by them.

The Word in itself is dead; it is the Spirit that quickens it, and quickens by it. All the arguments which ministers may draw out of the Word in preaching, though pressed with never so much earnestness and affection, cannot possibly produce this gracious change in people unless God sets in with the Word and sets it home upon the heart. We may as easily tear hard rocks to pieces and bend great bars of iron with our breath as, by our preaching, break the stony hearts and bend the iron sinews in the necks of the impenitent. We may as easily lift a mountain with one finger and toss it up to heaven, or, with a whisper, raise those who are dead in their graves as lift a carnal heart towards God and raise such as are spiritually dead, unless the Lord accompanies the Word which we preach with the Holy Ghost from heaven (1 Peter 1:12).

If we bring the light to a carnal man, a hard-hearted sinner, open it in his face and tell him never so convincingly of his sin, his guilt, the curse of the law, the wrath of God, the damnation of hell, and what dreadful torments he is hastening towards in his sinful courses, yet he is insensible and secure, and not at all moved unless it is with anger against the minister who reproves and forewarns him of his danger. And, notwithstanding all that can be said, he goes on resolvedly in this way, which will certainly and may suddenly bring him to hell. Or, if he trembles a little with Felix, if some slavish fear of punishment arises in him for the present through the impression of arguments upon natural conscience, yet however he hears sin aggravated as it reflects dishonor upon God and defiles his own soul, he is not moved to the least true, godly, evangelical mourning and sorrow for it.

Let us set God forth in His glorious excellencies and perfections before such a sinner in His infinite greatness, power, holiness, wisdom, goodness, truth, faithfulness, mercy, and lovingkindness, yet we cannot persuade him to fear God filially, to desire Him truly, to love Him entirely, or to choose Him for his chief good here and his portion eternally.

Let us set forth the Lord Jesus Christ in His beauty
and transcendent loveliness, in His mercy and incomparable grace and love; let us speak to him
never so undeniably of the great need which he has
of Christ to be his Savior because he is a sinner, and
in such danger because of sin; let us call upon him
never so earnestly, entreat him never so pathetically
to leave his sin and accept Christ so freely offered
unto him; not he! He holds fast to his sin; he shuts
his ear like the deaf adder who will not hear the
voice of the charmer though he charms ever so
wisely. And when he harbors base lusts in his heart,
which will destroy him, he shuts the door against
Jesus Christ, although he might have pardon and
salvation, grace and glory with Him.

Let us propound to him ever so clearly the
grounds of faith; let us direct him, invite him, and
persuade him to believe with the greatest possible
Scripture encouragements, and yet as easily may we
persuade him to lift up the earth in his arms as to
put forth the least true act of faith. Let us commend
to him the ways of God with the highest praises, and
call him into those ways with the most powerful motives of peace, satisfaction, sweetness, advantage
here, and happiness to eternity; and yet nothing will
prevail with him to set one step into that path.

Surely, then, there is no inherent virtue in the
Word, or any arguments, though never so persua-
sive, to effect this good work of grace. Indeed, we
must urge and press arguments upon sinners to dis-
suade them from sin and draw them to God and this
holy path, because God works upon rational creatures in a rational way; yet all arguments are in

themselves insufficient to produce this work, as we
find by the different effects which the very same arguments make on those upon whom they are urged.
Some are moved, repent, and turn to God; others are
obdurate, obstinate, and continue in their impeni-
tency and way of disobedience whatever is said
against them. Yea, some who are more unlikely to be
wrought upon, more defiled and hardened before,
when also they have resisted and withstood stronger
arguments, have afterwards yielded and been overcome, and have fallen down before the force which
has accompanied weaker arguments. This difference in the operation of the Word plainly shows
that this work of grace is not from the Word, however preached and pressed, but from the power of
God's Spirit. All that has been said to the negative
makes way and proves also the positive.

Positively, God alone is the Author of the good
work of grace. It is God who begins the work, and it
is God who performs it. In this work we are born
again (John 3:3), and we are said to be both begotten of God (James 1:18: "Of His own will begat He us
by the word of truth") and to be born of God (John
1:13: "Which are born, not of blood, nor of the will
of flesh, nor of the will of man, but of God"; and
1 John 4:7: "Whosoever loveth is born of God"). We
can no more beget ourselves anew than we can
beget ourselves in our birth; it is a supernatural
work, and therefore can be effected by none but
God, who is almighty; who, by an immediate and
real influence upon the soul, effects a spiritual
change whereby all the faculties are changed, not in
regard of their essence, but in regard of their quali-

fications. In this work lions are turned into lambs,
wolves into sheep, stones into flesh, yea, into children of Abraham. What I mean here is that the
fierce and ravenous disposition is changed into a
mild and gentle temper; the stony obdurateness is
removed, and the heart, which was as hard as flint
before, is made soft and pliable to the will and law of
God. And who can do this but the God of nature,
who first formed the spirit within man, and who
alone can newly form and newly mold it after His
own image?

This good work is called "a new creation" in
Ephesians 2:10: "We are His workmanship, created
in Jesus Christ unto good works." Ephesians 4:24:
"Put on the new man, which after God is created in
righteousness and true holiness." And therefore
such as have this work done in them are called new
creatures in 2 Corinthians 5:17: "If any man be in
Christ, he is a new creature; old things are passed
away, behold all things are become new." And then
it follows in the next verse: "All things are of God."
All these new things are His more immediate work.
It was God alone who created all things at first and it
is God alone who can create all things anew.

This work of grace is called "a resurrection," and
hereby sinners are quickened out of their spiritual
death (Ephesians 2:1). It is God who gives natural
life, and He alone can give spiritual life. He raised
Christ from the dead on the third day, and He will
raise up all who are dead on the last day; and only
He can raise up a soul when it is dead in sin and
quicken it by His Spirit, which requires the same
power as was put forth in Christ's resurrection

(compare Ephesians 1:19–20 with Ephesians 2:5). God indeed makes use of the Word in quickening and changing the soul, but the Word effects this work only instrumentally—God works it efficiently. As there went forth a power with Christ's Word when He called and raised Lazarus from the dead (John 11:42–43), so the power of God's Spirit goes forth with the Word of His grace to quicken dead souls and effect a gracious change within them.

Section 4

*Why does the Lord begin this good work
in any of the children of men?*

The reason, as to the motive, is only God's free grace and love. The reason, as to the design and end, is partly that God might be glorified by them upon earth, and partly that they might be prepared for glory with Him forever in heaven.

The motive which induces God to begin this good work in any of the children of men is only His free grace and love. It is a gracious work of God not only with regard to the grace which it effects, but also with regard to the grace from whence it proceeds. It is according to the good pleasure of God's will that He chooses us (Ephesians 1:5), and it is according to the good pleasure of His will that He changes us (James 1:18).

Natural agents, in producing effects, act necessarily. God is a voluntary agent, and in this work acts freely. Ephesians 2:4–5: "God who is rich in mercy, for His great love wherewith He hath loved us, even when we were dead in sins, hath quickened us together with Christ." Romans 9:15: "For He saith unto Moses, 'I will have mercy on whom I will have mercy, and compassion on whom I will have compassion.' " If God hides the mysteries of salvation from the wise and prudent, suffering them to remain in a dark and unconverted state, and reveals those mysteries unto babes; if He chooses and calls the foolish, mean, and most despised persons, and puts His image and likeness upon them, we must say that nothing but free grace could move Him thereunto. And then we must, with our Savior, acknowledge, "Even so Father, for so it seemed good in Thy sight" (Matthew 11:26).

And not only when the most unlikely person, the ignorant or notoriously wicked, is graciously changed must we cry out "Grace! Grace!" but also, whoever they are, however morally qualified before conversion, there is not the least merit in any of their works, nothing to move or incline God unto it, no disposition in the nature of any unto this gracious change. And therefore it is only of free grace that those who have escaped the more gross pollutions which are in this world through lust are washed by the Spirit in the laver of regeneration from the inward pollutions of their hearts, from which none are free. Titus 3:4–5: "But after that the kindness and love of God our Savior toward man appeared. Not by works of righteousness which we have done, but according to His mercy He saved us, by the washing of regeneration and renewing of the Holy Ghost." And 2 Timothy 1:9: "Who hath saved us, and called us with a holy calling, not according to our works, but according to His own will and purpose."

The design and end why God begins the good work of grace in any of the children of men is:

1. That hereby they might be fitted for His service, and glorify His name upon the earth. All grace-

less persons are not only children of wrath, but children of disobedience. They are children of darkness and of the devil, yea, they are his servants; they serve the devil and divers lusts, and their whole life is a continual offense and provocation of God, a continued course of rebellion against Him and His laws. The Lord therefore brings some of the children of men out of a state of nature into a state of grace that He might have some servants in the world, some to bear His name and stand up for His honor and interest, and oppose the sins of the times and places wherein they live; that He might have some service from them. Hebrews 12:28: "Let us have grace that we may serve God acceptably." Without a work of grace upon the heart and a sanctified principle within, no services are acceptable unto God, "for they that are in the flesh cannot please God" (Romans 8:8).

2. That hereby they might be fitted for glory with God forever in heaven. God gives grace here to prepare for glory hereafter. Only the pure in heart are fit and have the promise of seeing God (Matthew 5:8). Without a new heart and life, there will be no admission into the new Jerusalem (Revelation 21:27). God is glorious in holiness, clothed with majesty, all brightness, perfect purity, the high and Holy One of Israel who inhabits eternity, without the least spot, and with whom dwells no iniquity. The heavens are not pure in His sight, and He has charged His angels with folly. The pure seraphim proclaim His holiness and veil their faces before the splendor thereof.

And this God who is so infinitely pure and holy

Himself infinitely hates and detests sin. There is an infinite contrarity between the holy nature of God and the unholy nature of man; and therefore they cannot live together with eternal delight in heaven unless the nature of man is changed by the renewing grace of God. God will not permit unsanctified persons to approach so near His glorious presence. He will not receive such defiled creatures into the dearest and closest embraces of His infinite and eternal love. And while they are unrenewed, heaven (which is a place of holiness whose company and employments are all holy) would be so unsuitable unto their natures that they could not find sweetness and delight there because none can delight in anything unless it has a suitableness to the nature of that thing in which they delight. Therefore the Lord changes the nature of such persons here in a work of grace whom He intends for eternal glory in the other world.

Section 5

The first use

Test yourselves whether this good work of grace has begun in you. You have seen many works of men before you. See whether this work of God is wrought in you. You have read of the work of grace, you have heard of the work of grace, and you have seen the effects of the work of grace in others; now search whether you can find the marks of this work in yourselves.

If the good work is begun in you, God has wrought in you a sense of your lost estate while in a state of nature. God has opened your eyes to perceive your guilt of sin and has stopped your mouths as to any plea or excuse. He has awakened your conscience to a sense of your danger, and that of everlasting ruin, while under the guilt of any unpardoned sin. The law has told you that "the soul that sinneth shall die" (Ezekiel 18:4). Conscience has told you that you have sinned, and the Spirit has made the conclusion that therefore you shall die. The law has told you, "Cursed is everyone that continueth not in all things which are written in the book of the law, to do them" (Galatians 3:10). Conscience has told you that you have neither continued nor done those things which are written in the law, but have broken it in such a point by profanity, and in such a point by uncleanness, and in such a point by drunkenness, and in such a point by

25

unrighteousness, and in every point by some act or another of disobedience. And the Spirit then has made the application that therefore you are cursed.

The gospel has told you that unless you repent you shall perish (Luke 13:3). Conscience has told you that you have not repented, and the Spirit has from this inferred that you shall perish. The gospel has told you that "he that believeth not is condemned already, and the wrath of God abideth on him" (John 3:18, 36). Conscience has told you that you have not believed, and the Spirit has applied it: therefore you are condemned and the wrath of God abides on you. The gospel has told you that Christ will come "in flaming fire to take vengeance on them that obey not the gospel," and that He will "punish them with everlasting destruction" (2 Thessalonians 1:8–9). Conscience has told you that you have not obeyed the gospel, and God, by His Spirit, has drawn the conclusion that therefore Christ will come in flaming fire to take vengeance upon you, and to everlastingly destroy you in hell for your disobedience.

Thus, when the Lord begins this good work, He convinces the sinner of his sin and his liability to the stroke of His vengeance, and works him to a sense of his lost state so that he cries out, "Oh, wretched man that I am! I have sinned, and woe to me. I must die, and that eternally! I must perish, and that everlastingly! The course I take will bring me to hell ere long. I have been treasuring up sin, and God has been treasuring up wrath for me. I have been pursuing inquity, and God is pursuing me with His vengeance. I have been taking pleasure in sin. I

have been merry and secure. I have frolicked and put
the evil day far from me; but pain and horror abide
for me and the evil day is drawing near and hastens
quickly—the day of wrath and vengeance, the day of
accounts when I must be judged and condemned
and punished in flames of everlasting fire for my
sins. And who can stand in that day? Who can endure God's anger? Who can dwell with devouring
fire? Now woe to me that I was ever born!" Have you
had such a sense as this of your lost state wrought in
you by God?

If the good work of grace is begun in you, God
has brought you to earnestly inquire what to do to
get out of this state. Thus the Jews who had imbrued
their hands in the blood of Christ afterwards were
"pricked in their hearts, and cried out, 'Men and
brethren, what shall we do?' " (Acts 2:37). Thus the
jailer, after he had scourged the apostles and thrust
them into the inner prison and put their feet into
the stocks, is struck with trembling by the earth-
quake and cries out, "Sirs, what must I do to be
saved?" (Acts 16:30).

When God gives a sense to sinners of their lost
estate in order to a gracious change, He does not
suffer them to abide there, but He stirs them up to
seek after a remedy and a way for recovery out of that
estate, and for the prevention of their future misery.
Some indeed lose their convictions and cast off
their troubles, and either shut their ears against the
clamors of their accusing conscience or in some
way or another stop the mouth of conscience so that
they may not be molested by it. But God will not
permit this to be in those whom He will bring home

effectually to Himself. He follows them with a light
in one hand to show them their sins, and with a
sword in the other hand to take vengeance upon
them. He meets them as the angel did Balaam:
wherever they turn He lets them know that if they
will venture to go on in that way they shall be slain.

Then they begin to think to themselves and
make inquiry of others how they may escape; and if
they could find help in any creature they would go
no further; if they could find any righteousness of
their own to present God with they would take up
with that. But God convinces them that they can
bring nothing to Him which can find any acceptance with Him, and this puts them at a great loss,
especially such as are unacquainted with the gospel
and the way of salvation by Jesus Christ. But withal
they are the more effectually prepared for a ready
closure with Jesus Christ when He is made known
and freely offered unto them. Have you ever had
such solicitousness and made such earnest inquiry
after the way of getting out of your lost state?

If God has begun the good work in you, He has
brought you to a grief and hatred of sin; and in
working this God reveals not only the mischief and
misery which sin will bring upon the sinner, but
also His love and tender mercy in His Son, and His
readiness to forgive and save. And this most kindly
melts and mollifies the heart when the sinner perceives that the offended God is ready to be reconciled, and has been at great cost, even the expense of
His Son's blood, to make provision for the sinner's
salvation. Hereby he is brought to the most bitter
grief for sin, and to the greatest loathing and

detestation of sin, beyond all other things in the
world. Now he cries out more about his sin than his
punishment; and he did not before entertain sin
with more readiness than he now rejects it with
abhorrence. He desires to be saved from sin more
than to be saved from hell.

If God has begun the good work in you, He has
wrought in you hungering desires after Jesus Christ.
When sin becomes most odious to the sinner, then
Christ becomes most precious; when sin is bitter,
then Christ is sweet; when sin is burdensome, then
Christ is desirable, who alone can remove this bur-
den. It is the sense of sickness which puts the dis-
eased person upon sending for the physician, and
the sense of the sickness of sin draws forth desires
after Christ, the great Soul-Physician. Then "None
but Christ, none but Christ!" is the breath of their
desire. "Oh, that Christ would come to me! Oh, that
Christ would undertake for me! Oh, that I could
have a sight of Him! Oh, that I could meet with
Him! Oh, that I had an interest in Him! Lord, give
me an interest in Thy Son! Thou hast given Him for
sinners. I am a sinner; give Him unto me! No one
has more need of Him. Oh, do not deny Him to me!
Deny me anything, but do not deny me Christ! Give
me Christ and I will have enough! Give me Christ
and I have all! Give me Christ or else I die and perish eternally!"

Have you had such breathings of desire after
Jesus Christ, and Him to sanctify you as well as to
save you? To heal you as well as to reconcile you?
Then be sure the work is begun.

If God has begun the good work in you, He has

wrought faith in you to lay hold of Christ. God holds forth His bleeding Son to the broken and bleeding-hearted sinner, and by His Spirit He draws him unto Himself. By His almighty power He draws him against the opposition of Satan and the flesh, enabling him to quit all other holds and lay hold of Christ. He is taken off his own foundation and builds all his hopes upon this Rock. He renounces his own righteousness and accepts the perfect righteousness which in Christ is provided for him and offered to him. And hereby alone he looks for remission of sin and acceptance with the Father. And if he cannot presently arrive at a confidence of his salvation, yet he ventures himself upon Christ and resolves that if he perishes he will perish endeavoring at least to trust in Him. Can you experience such a work of faith as this?

If God has begun the good work in you, then He has worked the love of Himself into your hearts. When the sinner has attained union with Christ by faith, this faith puts forth itself in the acts of most sincere and supreme love and affection unto God. Now God is chosen as the chief Good, and the highest room in the heart is given unto Him. The believer has love for other things, but God is loved in all of them. God is loved above all of them. Now this person loves God for His Son, and he loves Him for Himself. He loves Him for His loveliness, and he loves Him for His love. He loves His image also wherever he sees it. He loves not only His goodness and mercy, but also His holiness and purity; and not only that which is in His person, but also that which is written in His law, and that which is engraven, though more imperfectly, upon His children. Have you such a love to God?

If God has begun the good work in you, then He has brought your heart unto a contempt of the world. The world appears to the believer to be a windy vanity in separation from God, and a vain, empty nothing in comparison to God. All earthly things in themselves are to him like a feather without weight, like a shadow without substance, like a breast without milk, like a cloud without rain, like a vapor which appears for a little while and soon vanishes away; and therefore he will not set his eyes and heart upon such things which are not what they seem to be, and are taking the wing so soon to be gone, and cease to be what they are. His eyes are upon a better and more enduring substance in comparison with which he esteems the world as a toy. Is the world thus brought down in your esteem?

And, lastly, if God has begun the good work in you, then He has brought you into a self-resignation and self-dedication unto Him. Believers look upon themselves as no longer their own, having made themselves over to God and devoted themselves unto His service. Other lords have had dominion over them. Sin has reigned and the devil has tyrannized; but now they are made free from sin and delivered from the power of Satan, and have yielded themselves up to God to give ready obedience to whatsoever He reveals to be His will and command.

Examine yourselves in these particulars, and you may know by this way of God's working whether the good work is begun in you.

Section 6

The second use

I might make other uses at this point, but I shall only add a use of exhortation to all who are without this good work, especially to you who are young, that now, in the beginning of your life, you would endeavor that this good work of grace may be begun in you.

I am glad to see so many of your faces together here on earth. I would rejoice more to see all your faces in heaven. I am glad to see you together in this house. I would rejoice more to see you all in God's family. God has blessed my ministry in the conversion of some among you, and the good work of grace has begun in you by a most unworthy and most unlikely instrument. Oh, that my ministry might be further blessed in the conversion of the rest who are unconverted! Oh, that I might be an instrument to begin the good work of grace in the heart of every graceless young man and young woman in this place! God, by His providence, has brought you to hear. Oh, that by His Spirit He would work and persuade you to repent and believe!

You are now under the dews of God's Word. Oh, that you might be under the influences of His grace; that while the seed of the Word is sowing in your ears that the seed of grace might be thrown into your hearts! Oh, that God would speak to you, that while His minister is speaking to you audibly that

God would speak to you feelingly and say, "Here's grace for you, young woman; here's repentance for you, sinner; and here's faith for you, unbeliever. Here's light and eyes for you who are blind; here's life and quickening for you who are dead in sins and trespasses." Oh, that you might hear God's thundering voice to awaken you who are asleep in sin, and then His still and sweet voice to allure you to His Son!

Some of you, though you are but young men and women, are yet old sinners. You have strong bodies, but you have stronger lusts. Some of you are not only apprentices unto men, but you are apprentices to the devil and have been bound to him ever since you were born. You have served him, some of you, for 15–20 years. Some of the older ones here have served the devil and their own lusts for nearly 50 years, and is it not time to be made free? Can you be well pleased with this service, which is so base a vassalage? Can you like the devil as your master? Can you love those bonds which enslave your souls, your most noble and excellent part, and by which the devil is leading you to hell? The devil rules over and works in all you who are children of disobedience; and is it not better to have Christ rule over you, and God work in you by His Spirit, when Christ's service is perfect freedom and God's work is the good work of grace?

Who knows but this may be the time and place wherein some captive souls may be made free and rescued by Christ out of the snares of Satan! And "if the Son shall make you free, you shall be free indeed" (John 8:36). Who knows but while I am speaking to you God may be working in you; and if God

will work, who can stop Him? Satan shall not stop
Him; sin shall not stop Him; the world shall not
stop Him. God may now create the fruit of the lips:
"Grace! Grace!" God can make the stoutest sinner to
tremble and the proudest sinner to stoop. He can
break the hardest rock and bow the iron sinew. He
can melt and soften the most obdurate heart. Oh,
that He would put forth His almighty arm and lay
hold upon your hearts, and, overturning the strong-
holds of His enemies within you, that He would
bring you into captivity and obedience to His Son!

Young ones, look up to God for a gracious
change now. Some of you are desirous to change
your condition; look up to God to change your nature. Some of you are looking out for new houses;
oh, that you would look up to God for new hearts!
There are many who say, "Who will show us any
good?" Rather say, "Lord, Thou hast shown us what
is good; work in us this good work of grace."

First, consider the necessity of it:

1. Without this good work of grace you have no
good in you. You have darkness instead of light, deformity instead of beauty, filthiness instead of purity,
love of the world instead of love to God, and the fire
of lust instead of the fire of zeal for God's glory.

2. Without this good work of grace, no good can
be done by you. You can do nothing but sin without
a sanctified principle of grace. Without life there
can be no vital operations, and without grace there
can be no gracious actions. If there is no good in
the root, there can be no good in the fruit; and if
there is no good in the heart, there can be no good
in the life. They that are in the flesh cannot please

God (Romans 8:8).

3. Without this good work of grace, no good belongs to you. There are many high and excellent privileges, many sweet and precious promises that belong to the gracious: election, adoption, remission of sins, salvation, and an audience for prayer. Plus, "all things shall work together for good for those that love God and are called according to His purpose" (Romans 8:28). But if you are without the good work of grace, you cannot lay claim to any gospel privilege, to any gospel promise; instead of being the children of God, you are the children of the devil; instead of the pardon of sin, your guilt still remains; instead of the audience of prayer, your prayers are an abomination; instead of all things working together for your good, all things work together for your hurt.

4. Without this good work of grace, there is no good laid up for you. God has laid *out* much for His people, but He has laid *up* more. Psalm 31:19: "O how great is Thy goodness, which Thou hast laid up for them that fear Thee!" 1 Corinthians 2:9: "Eye hath not seen, nor ear heard, neither hath entered into the heart of man the things which God hath prepared for them that love Him." God has set forth these things by treasures, joys, crowns, an exceeding and eternal weight of glory; yet when all is said and done, these things exceed all comparison and comprehension. But without the good work, none of these things are prepared and laid up for you. Treasures are indeed laid up for you, but they are treasures of wrath; a portion is prepared, but it is fire and brimstone, and a horrible tempest will be this

portion. There will be no admission for you into
heaven without grace, and then I need not tell you
that you must take up your lodging forever among
devils in the unquenchable flames of hell.

Second, consider the excellency of this work. It is
an excellent work which requires so excellent a
worker to effect it; and that is God, who works it by
the immediate influence of His Spirit. It is an excellent work which so ennobles the spirit of man, who
so beautifies the soul, which is the renewing of
God's lost image, which is the engraving of God's
Spirit. It is an excellent work which furnishes the
heart and makes it fit to be a habitation for God by
His Spirit, which brings the creature into fellowship
with the Father and the Son. It is an excellent work
which is heaven begun, glory in the bud, happiness
in the first fruit, the inheritance in the earnest
penny, and which qualifies for, as well as is the beginning of, eternal life.

Third, consider that this good work of grace is
attainable, and that by you, whoever you are. Though
you are never so mean in parts, though ignorant
and unlearned in condition, though poor and without land or money, though never so vile and great a
sinner, though you have no righteousness or merit
unless it is of death and hell, yet, since grace is free
and God gives it freely without respect of persons or
anything in persons, any of you are capable of it and
it is attainable by you.

Fourth, consider that it is the most seasonable
time for you to get grace while you are still young.
Now God is most ready to give it; you will be most
ready to receive it before your conscience is grown

more seared, your hearts more hardened, and your lusts more strengthcned; before you are more entangled in the world, more defiled with sin, and more captivated by the devil. Few who refuse the offers of grace when they are young accept it when they are old. Now is the accepted time; the day of life may be at an end or the day of grace may be at an end before you are aware. Delay no longer. Harken to the present call. Take a view of your sins in the glass which God holds forth unto you. Look upwards to the frowns of God upon you; look inward to the wounds of conscience within you; look forward to death and judgment which are hastening upon you; and look downward to the punishment of hell which is preparing for you even now unless you repent and turn to the Lord.

Labor for a sense of your danger, a feeling of sin's power, and a loathing of sin's defilement. And then look to Christ, who alone can save you from misery and from your iniquity; lay hold on Him. In your endeavor, God may work and help you to repent and believe. And once this good work is begun in you, you would not be without it for ten thousand worlds. Be sure then you do not perish or miss everlasting happiness, because He who has begun the good work will perform it till the day of Christ, which leads us to the second doctrine.

Section 7

The second doctrine: the good work which God begins in the day of grace He will perform until the day of Christ

I n handling this point, I shall: (1) speak concerning the day of grace wherein God begins the good work; (2) speak concerning God's performing this good work which He begins; (3) speak concerning the day of Christ until which God will perform the good work; (4) prove that God will perform the good work until the day of Christ; (5) answer some objections; and (6) make application.

1. Concerning the day of grace wherein God begins the good work: by the day of grace we are to understand any time in this life wherein the Lord makes offers of grace wherein He calls sinners to repentance and invites them to His Son so that they might attain remission and salvation by Him. This day of grace is any time in this life, and this life only; for there is no day of grace in another life. There is a day of glory for the gracious, but no day of grace for sinners; there is a day of wrath for sinners, but no day of grace. The day of grace for sinners is only in this life, while they have the means of grace, which is called "the accepted time and the day of salvation" (2 Corinthians 6:2). In this day of grace the Lord begins the good work in all those who be-

long unto the election of grace. He not only offers grace, but bestows it; in their hearing the word of grace, they attain the good work of grace. While God calls them externally by the preaching of the Word, He calls them effectually, and works a gracious change in them by the operations of His Spirit. And so the good work is begun, of which I have spoken at length under the first doctrine.

2. Concerning God's performing the good work which He has begun, the word in the original signifies "to finish or bring to perfection." It includes God's carrying on the good work of grace so that it shall never quite fail, nor shall those who have it totally fall from it.

3. Concerning the day of Christ, until which God will perform the good work of grace which He has begun: The day of Christ is sometimes in Scripture taken for the day of His bodily presence with His disciples here on earth, which is past. And though He foretells His disciples that they will, after His departure, desire one of those days of His bodily presence to comfort them under the afflictions which they must endure for His sake, yet no such day would be seen by them. Luke 17:22: "And He said unto His disciples, 'The days will come when ye shall desire to see one of the days of the Son of Man, and ye shall not see it.' " But the day of Christ here spoken of is the day which is to come, not that which is past; it is the day of the second appearance of Christ in His glory, not the day of His first appearance in a state of humiliation; it is the last day, when the Lord Jesus will come down from heaven to judge the whole world. God will perform the good work of grace

which He has begun in the gracious ones until this day of Christ's appearance; not as if then their grace should fail, but then it shall arrive unto its full perfection and lodge them safely in the arms of their Savior and in the eternal embraces of His love.

It is through God's performance of this good work begun in His people that they will be blameless in the day of Christ, and that they will be qualified for a reception into habitations of everlasting blessedness. 1 Corinthians 1:8: "Who shall confirm you unto the end, that ye may be blameless in the day of our Lord Jesus Christ." 1 Thessalonians 5:23: "And the very God of peace sanctify you wholly, and I pray God your whole spirit, and soul, and body be preserved unto the coming of our Lord Jesus Christ."

Section 8

The fourth particular

The fourth and chief particular which I shall speak to is to prove that God will perform the good work which He has begun until the day of Christ; that He will never allow grace begun to fail till it arrives to perfection. The truly gracious person shall persevere unto the end, and shall never finally nor totally fall away.

Before I come to prove the point, I shall premise a few things for a better understanding thereof:

1. Concerning the good work which God will perform and not suffer quite to fail: I am not speaking of the work itself, such as conviction, contrition, some kind of trouble for sin and the like, which many may have and totally lose so as never to gain them any more. I am speaking of the good work of grace in the truth of it, not of the counterfeit work which too many hypocrites have and from which they may totally fall. I am speaking of the special work of grace, not of the common gifts and illuminations and spiritual tastes which may be given by the Spirit to some who are unsound, from which they may totally apostatize into the unpardonable sin against the Holy Ghost so as never to be renewed again unto repentance.

2. Concerning God's performing of the good work: I don't say that the gracious themselves can perform it, but that if they should be left to them-

selves they would fall away both totally and finally. But God has undertaken to perform it, and to help them from falling away; and He will do it. I don't say that God will perform this good work in any in their neglect of the means for their establishment and perseverance, and in any licentious course which they may take, but He will perform it in the diligent use of the means appointed by Him, and their refraining from sin in which, if they should indulge themselves, they would be cut off from His favor and bring unavoidable and eternal death upon themselves. Romans 8:13: "If ye live after the flesh, ye shall die." This was spoken by the Apostle to the believing Romans.

3. Concerning the failing of the work: I don't say but the work of grace begun may fail in regard of the vigorous exercise of it; such acts may be suspended at some times. Nor do I say that the habits of grace may not fail in regard of some degrees of strength. Gracious persons may be under declinings and decays of grace (of which I shall speak more when I come to the caution), but the habits of grace shall never wholly fail. The life remains in the root when the fruit falls off and only a few leaves remain.

Having premised these things, I come now to prove that God will perform the good work of grace which He has begun, or that true grace shall never quite fail, nor true saints ever totally fall from grace. And this will appear from God's election and calling them, and from God's covenant and promise to them.

From God's election and calling of such as are

gracious, it appears that He will perform the good work which He has begun in them so that they shall never totally fall. God has elected and chosen all such as are gracious from before the foundation of the world unto eternal salvation by an absolute, infallible, immutable decree. He has chosen them to grace here and glory hereafter; and by grace to fit them for glory, by holiness in this world to fit them for happiness in the other world. And therefore they shall never totally or finally fall from grace, which is absolutely necessary to bring them to glory.

The perseverance of the saints, or the gracious, may be thus proven from election. If there is an absolute and immutable decree of election whereby a particular number of men and woman are chosen unto salvation; if all those who are particularly elected shall infallibly and most certainly attain that salvation to which they are chosen; if none can attain salvation without grace, and perseverance in grace, but are brought unto it thereby; if all the saints, or such who have the work of grace begun in them, are elected, or are in the number of those who are chosen to salvation, and, by consequence, shall certainly attain salvation, and that by perseverance in grace; then it must follow undeniably that the saints or gracious persons shall certainly persevere and never fall totally from grace. But these things are so, as I shall show in each particular, and therefore the consequence is certain.

1. There is an absolute eternal and immutable decree of election whereby a particular number of men and women are chosen unto salvation. This is evident from Scripture, which speaks of this decree

as being from before the foundation of the world
(Ephesians 1:4: "According as He hath chosen us in
Him before the foundation of the world"), and of
God's purpose of election before the particular per-
sons chosen are born, without respect to their
works, but only to His own will (Romans 9:11, 13:
"For the children being not yet born, neither hav-
ing done good or evil, that the purpose of God ac-
cording to election might stand, not of works, but of
Him that calleth: It was said, 'Jacob have I loved, but
Esau have I hated' ").

Moreover, besides this express Scripture, there is
reason that God's decree of election should be absolute and immutable, not depending upon the muta-
ble will of man, or any foreseen works to move Him
herein, because God forsees nothing as future but
what He has decreed, and nothing to come to pass
in time could move God's will before time insomuch as His will is the cause of whatever is future,
and not anything that is future is the cause of God's
will, unless something that is temporal could be the
cause of that which is eternal, which is absurd. God
knows from eternity all possible things that never
come to pass, but He knows no future things but as
He will that they should come to pass; insomuch as
nothing can rationally be imagined should bring
them out of the number of possible things into the
number of certain future things but the will and
decree of God. Therefore God's decree of election
must be absolute, certain, and immutable.

2. Hence it follows that all those who are particularly elected shall infallibly and most certainly attain that salvation which they are chosen unto,

otherwise God's decree would not be certain. And it would argue a weakness in God if He should from eternity purpose and resolve to do a thing which He should never bring to pass. But this cannot be ascribed to God, who is infinite in power and powerfully "worketh all things according to the counsel of His will" (Ephesians 1:11). God can as soon cease to be God as not effect what He has eternally purposed, because He would cease to be unchangeable, which is His essential property. Therefore, as sure as God is God, all the elect shall be saved.

3. None can attain salvation without grace and perseverance therein who are not brought thereunto by it. 2 Thessalonians 2:13: "But we are bound to give thanks always unto God for you, brethren, beloved of God, because God hath from the beginning chosen you unto salvation through sanctification of the Spirit and belief of the truth." Without faith and sanctification, there is no possibility of attaining salvation. God has appointed sanctification to be the means without which salvation, which is the end, cannot be attained. And not only the grace of sanctification is necessary to salvation, but also perseverance in this grace to the end. Matthew 24:13: "He that endureth to the end shall be saved." Revelation 2:10: "Be thou faithful unto death, and I will give thee a crown of life."

4. All the saints or gracious persons who have the good work begun in them are elect and in the number of those particular persons who are chosen unto salvation. This is evident because the grace begun in them is the fruit of election. Acts 13:48: "As many as were ordained to eternal life believed." The grace of

faith is the fruit of ordination or election unto eternal life. So Ephesians 1:4: "He hath chosen us that we should be holy." Therefore, if any are holy, it is because they are chosen or elected. As whom God has chosen to the end, which is salvation and eternal happiness, He has also chosen the means, which is sanctification and holiness, so whom He has chosen to the means, He has chosen to the end.

Hence, then, it is strongly and undeniably necessary that gracious persons—being chosen to salvation, which they shall certainly attain unto, and that by the means of grace and perseverance therein—shall persevere in grace to the end, and never totally and finally fall from it.

I shall here add one Scripture which joins election, grace, and glory together, whereby will plainly appear the perseverance of the gracious. Romans 8:30: "Whom He did predestinate, them He also called; whom He called, them He also justified; whom He justified, them He also glorified." Here is the golden chain of man's salvation in its four great links: the first is predestination or election; the second is effectual calling or vocation; the third is justification; and the fourth is glorification. These God has joined together, and none can pluck them asunder. Some have attempted to do it, but it has never been done except in the fond imagination of some men.

God has here coupled and linked predestination and calling, then calling and justification, then justification and glorification; and they hang so together that they cannot be divided. Now if true grace should quite fail, and the good work which God has begun come to nothing, then one link of this chain would be broken off, and that is effectual calling, which is none other than the good work of grace begun. I say, effectual calling, then, would be broken off from God's election, and election would be uncertain. Then God's decree would be immutable, the impossibility of which I have already proven.

Moreover, effectual calling, if true grace could fail, would be broken off from justification, unless God should give to such a pardon and retract it afterwards again. Be sure it would be broken off from glorification, for those who fall from grace will fall short of heaven. But the links are strong and cannot be broken; therefore true grace shall never quite fail.

And here I shall join one or two arguments from effectual calling itself to prove that gracious persons shall never totally and finally fall. Those whom God has effectually called, He has called to glory. 1 Thessalonians 2:12: "That ye would walk worthy of Him who hath called you unto His kingdom and glory." And as to whom He effectually calls to grace He gives grace, so to whom He effectually calls to glory He will give glory. He has given them the beginnings of it, and He will bring those beginnings unto perfection.

Moreover, God's gifts of grace and His effectual calling of the gracious is without repentance. Romans 11:29: "The gifts and calling of God are without repentance." But if gracious persons could totally fall from grace, God's gifts and calling would not be without repentance; therefore they cannot totally fall.

Section 9

The second argument proving that gracious persons shall never fall from the good work begun in them

The second argument to prove that gracious persons shall never fall from the good work begun in them may be drawn from God's covenant and promises which He has made unto them.

1. Such as are taken into an everlasting covenant shall never totally fall from grace. But all truly gracious persons are taken into an everlasting covenant, therefore they shall never totally fall from grace. That gracious persons are taken into covenant is evident because the grace of the covenant is wrought in them. That this covenant is everlasting is evident from Isaiah 55:3: "I will make an everlasting covenant with you, even the sure mercies of David." And from Jeremiah 32:40: "I will make an everlasting covenant with them." That such as are taken into an everlasting covenant shall never totally fall from grace is evident because their total fall from grace would turn them out of the covenant, inasmuch as it would turn them out of God's favor. And there is no promise of the covenant that belongs to total apostates—many threatenings, but no promises—and so the covenant would not be everlasting to them, neither would the mercies therefore be sure mercies.

2. Those to whom God has made sure promises of everlasting life and happiness shall never totally fall from grace. But God has made sure promises of everlasting life and happiness to all who are truly gracious; therefore none who are truly gracious shall totally fall from grace. That God has made sure promises of everlasting life and happiness unto those who are truly gracious is evident in the promises which He has made to faith (John 3:16: "Whosoever believeth in Him shall not perish, but have everlasting life." Acts 16:31: "Believe on the Lord Jesus Christ, and thou shalt be saved.") and in the promises He has made to love (1 Corinthians 2:9: "Eye hath not seen, nor ear heard, neither hath it entered into the heart of man, what God hath prepared for them that love Him." James 1:12: "He shall receive the crown of life, which God hath promised unto them that love Him.").

All such as are truly gracious have these graces of faith and love, and therefore the promises of eternal life and happiness are made unto them. That those to whom these promises are made shall not totally fall from grace is evident because, as has already been shown, if they should totally fall from grace they would fall short of heaven; therefore they shall not totally fall from grace.

OBJECTION. These promises of everlasting life are made only to those who persevere in grace to the end.

ANSWER. They are made unto all who are gracious without exception, and so carry in them an evident proof of their perseverance. God has moreover promised perseverance unto those who are gracious, which may be a third argument under this head.

3. Those to whom God has promised persever-ance shall never totally fall from grace. But God has promised perseverance unto all those who are truly gracious; therefore they shall never totally fall from grace. That those to whom God has promised perse-verance shall never totally fall from grace I suppose none will deny; for however some say, "God has promised life and happiness upon the condition of perseverance, yet they cannot assign any condition upon which God promises perseverance unless they make perseverance to be the condition of persever-ance. And so that God will enable His people to per-severe on the condition that they do persevere, and that He will keep them from falling on the condi-tion that they keep themselves from falling, is all very absurd.

That God has promised perseverance to all those who are gracious is evident in the covenant. Ezekiel 36:37: "And I will put My Spirit within you, and cause you to walk in My statutes, and ye shall keep My judgments and do them." This includes a promise not only of enabling His people to begin to keep His statutes, but also to continue to keep them and persevere unto the end. More plain is Jeremiah 32:40: "I will put My fear into their hearts, that they shall not depart from Me." God keeps His people from falling by His power through faith. 1 Peter 1:5: "Who are kept by the power of God through faith unto salvation." And He has promised to keep their faith and fulfill that work in them with power. This is included in Paul's prayer for the believing Thessalonians in 2 Thessalonians 1:11, that God would "fulfill all the good pleasure of His goodness, and the work of faith with power." Hence, then, it is clearly evident that truly gracious persons shall never totally fall from grace.

Section 10

*Objections and answers against the
perseverance of the saints*

The fifth thing is to answer some objections against the doctrine of the saints' perseverance, which may seem to prove that truly gracious persons may totally fall from the grace begun in them.

OBJECTION 1. Experience gives sufficient evidence of some saints who have fallen totally, though they have recovered again and not fallen finally. And the Scriptures witness the same when they tell us of Peter's denial of his Master and David's murder and adultery. How could such sins be consistent with a state of grace? Especially the last instance of David, who lay a long time before he recovered.

ANSWER 1. True saints and gracious persons may fall into sin, but they cannot fall from grace. They may fall foully, but they cannot fall totally; they may fall so as to break their bones, but they cannot fall so as to break their necks; they may sin themselves out of the sense of God's favor, but they shall never sin away His favor; they may sin so as to break their peace, but they shall never sin so as to provoke God to break His covenant; by their falls their graces may exceedingly decay, but they shall never be quite lost.

ANSWER 2. As for that example of Peter, it is evident from Scripture that though he fell into sin, and that a great sin, yet he did not fall from grace. For our Savior told him in Luke 22:32: "I have prayed for thee, that thy faith fail not." Be sure Christ's prayer was heard. And if Peter's faith did not quite fail, at least as to the habit of it, though it was interrupted as to the exercise of it, be sure the work of grace in him did not quite fail.

ANSWER 3. The same may be said of David. Though by his falls he lost the joys of God's salvation, yet he did not fall from a state of salvation; though the fruit which he brought forth before fell, yet the seed of grace still remained in him. The mercies of David were sure mercies, and, although God was displeased with David, yet He promised He would not utterly take away His lovingkindness from him (Psalm 89:34). And if he did not quite lose God's lovingkindness, surely he did not quite lose his own grace.

OBJECTION 2. But some eminent saints have fallen totally and finally too. Great pillars in the Church have not only trembled in shaking times, but tumbled. And some stars of heaven have fallen to the earth and never recovered their station again. The Scriptures tell us of Demas, who turned away from the ways of God, being allured by the present world; of Hymeneus and Alexander, who made shipwreck of the faith and put away a good conscience; of the turning away of Phygellus and Hermogenes; yea, of some who have been enlightened and tasted of the heavenly gift, and have been made partakers of the Holy Ghost and have tasted the good Word of

God and the powers of the world to come. Yet these, after all, have fallen quite away into the sin against the Holy Ghost, so that it has been impossible to renew them again to repentance.

ANSWER 1. None who ever had the good work of grace begun in them in truth ever fell like this, for the reasons which out of Scripture have been given.

ANSWER 2. Therefore, all those who have totally and finally fallen never really did, but only seemed to. Whatever pillars have tumbled were never built upon Christ the sure foundation; whatever stars have fallen were but comets, not real stars which never fall. However the lamp of some hypocrites may seem for a while to shine as brightly as others, yet they are without the oil of true grace in the vessel of their hearts; and it is no wonder that their lamps go out. They are hypocrites only who totally and finally fall. And it is but from counterfeit or common grace that they fall, which is plain from 1 John 2:19, where John speaks of the departure and apostasy of some professors: "They went out from us, but they were not of us, for if they had been of us, they would no doubt have continued with us, but they went out that they might be made manifest that they were not all of us."

These hypocrites who departed from the faith seemed to be true saints and disciples of Christ; and if they had been so indeed, no doubt, that is, most certainly, they would have continued and persevered. But by their apostasy they gave a manifest proof of their hypocrisy. Therefore, when the Apostle spoke of the apostasy of Hymeneus, who had not only fallen himself, but also overthrew the faith of others, he tells Timothy, "Nevertheless the foundation of God standeth sure, having this seal, 'The Lord knoweth them that are His' " (2 Timothy 2:19). Where God lays a foundation of true grace in the hearts of any, it is sure and cannot be overthrown; where God puts the seal of His Spirit upon any, it cannot be broken. Those whom God, by His seal, marks and owns as His, He will never disown, and they shall never quite fall away.

ANSWER 3. As to that faith which may be made shipwreck of and overthrown, it is not the grace of faith, but the profession of faith and the doctrine of faith which, in a storm of persecution, may be cast away and renounced by some. By strong delusions and believing lies they may be overthrown in others.

ANSWER 4. As to that good conscience which may be put away, it is not a truly good and sanctified conscience, but a moral and comparatively good conscience, such as Paul professed he had while he was a Pharisee before his conversion. This later may be put away, but not the former.

ANSWER 5. As to those enlightenings and tastes which some may quite lose and fall away from into the unpardonable sin, they are but common gifts of the Spirit, not special sanctifying grace.

OBJECTION 3. Ezekiel 18:24: "When the righteous turneth from his righteousness and committeth iniquity . . . he shall die."

ANSWER. Either the prophet is speaking of legal righteousness rather than evangelical, or some temporal untimely death rather than eternal; or, as I rather think, that he is speaking only by way of sup-

position, which shall never come to pass. An example of this would be Romans 8:13: "If ye live after the
flesh ye shall die." And yet he tells them that there
was no condemnation to them, that nothing could
separate them from the love of Christ; so that they
would neither live after the flesh nor die, though it
was true that if they lived after the flesh they *would*
die. So Galatians 1:8: "If an angel from heaven
preach another gospel, let him be accursed." It does
not hence follow that an angel from heaven would
or could preach another gospel, and so would be accursed (though an angel from hell might do it). So
when it says that if the righteous turns from his
righteousness he shall die, it does not follow that he
will turn from his righteousness and then die. But
the Lord makes use of threatenings and cautions, as
well as promises and other encouragements, to keep
the righteous from turning from his righteousness,
and all little enough sometimes for his establishment.

OBJECTION 4. This doctrine opens a door to licentiousness, for when any have true grace they may
think to themselves, "Let me do what I will, I shall
never perish. I am now out of all danger of eternal
death and wrath." And so they will be prone to indulge themselves in sin and a looser conversation.
Whereas the danger of falling away would be a
greater bridle and restraint upon them to keep them
from sin, and a greater spur to quicken them unto
watchfulness and constancy in holy duties.

ANSWER 1. God threatens the saints themselves
with eternal death and wrath if they turn from His

ways unto a vicious conversation; and no doubt but they would perish if they should do it (Romans 8:13).

ANSWER 2. The saints know that sin, if they presume to commit it, will at least break their peace, rob them of their comfort, and make havoc of their grace; therefore they fear to sin.

ANSWER 3. The promises of perseverance secure the gracious not only from falling into hell, but also from falling into a course of sin; and by these promises they are strengthened and enabled to stand when others, for lack of the help of them, fall.

ANSWER 4. Those who grow licentious upon presumption of their perseverance, it is a great symptom of their hypocrisy; and such are likely to fall quite away.

ANSWER 5. Those who are truly gracious are more ingenuous, and have more love to their heavenly Father, than to presume to sin against Him, and to fly in His face because He has promised He will not disinherit them.

ANSWER 6. As sin is opposed to grace, so grace is opposed to sin; and the more encouragement grace has, the more vigorous will it be in its opposition to sin. Experience tells us that in such gracious persons as have an assurance of God's love and perseverance are so far from taking occasion hereby for licentiousness that of all others they prove to be the most strict walking Christians.

Section 11

The application

Establish yourselves in the belief of this doctrine, that God will perform and perfect the good work of grace which He has begun, that the truly gracious shall persevere to the end and never either totally or finally fall.

USE 1. Take heed of entertaining that error which is contrary unto this great truth, which has such a clear and sure foundation in the Scriptures. Beware of such as hold that the saints may fall away, or who deny what is express in the text, that God will perform the good work begun until the day of Christ. For how does God perform the work if the work ceases and His people fall from grace? Such persons, in effect, say that God's decrees are uncertain, that His love is changeable, that His covenant may be broken, that His Word is unsure, that His promises are deceitful, that His Son's death might be in vain, that Christ's members might be torn off from His body and thrown into hell, that Christ's sheep might be lost so as never to be found again, that those whom Christ has loved and espoused may be divorced, hated, and at length found among the damned, and that the Holy Spirit might be quite expelled from His habitation and the devil get possession of His place. (For lack of room in these few pages, I was forced in the doctrinal part to leave out the arguments I had prepared to prove the saint's perseverance, drawn from these later considerations.) Take heed of such unscriptural, uncomfortable tenets. Those who hold them are great deniers of and enemies to the doctrine of God's free and distinguishing grace, and of the powerful working of God's Spirit, and hereby are the greatest enemies unto themselves and their own salvation.

Beware, therefore, of the leaven of this doctrine, which spreads itself in too many places. Never believe that one who is a child of God today may be a child of the devil tomorrow, that an heir of heaven today may be an heir of hell tomorrow. Hold fast and persevere in this truth: God will carry on the good work which He has begun until He has brought it to perfection, that true saints shall never totally and finally fall, but shall hold and persevere to the end. Believe firmly that all the gracious, being received into the arms of God's mercy, are kept by the hand of His power, and that His faithfulness, as well as their faith, is their shield; yea, that His faithfulness is the shield of their faith. Believe that none can pluck the gracious out of God's hand, and let none pluck this truth out of your mind. Let none persuade you to the contrary; not the devil, nor any of the children of darkness, as long as the Father of lights has so clearly revealed it in the Word.

USE 2. The work of grace being such a good work and so abiding, I think that all of you should be very inquisitive whether this good work is begun in you. Look and see whether you have any evidence to show for this good work. The wicked can show you the works of the flesh; can you show the works of the Spirit? In Galatians 5:19–21, the Apostle enu-

merates the works of the flesh: "Now the works of
the flesh are manifest, which are these: adultery,
fornication, uncleanness, lasciviousness, idolatry,
witchcraft, hatred, variance, emulations, wrath,
strife, seditions, envying, murders, drunkenness,
revellings, and such like, of which I tell you before,
as I have told you in times past, that they which do
such things shall not inherit the kingdom of God."
And therefore, such as do works as these are without
the good work of grace.

Are the works of the Spirit manifest in you, works
such as repentance, godly sorrow for sin, filial fear
of God, hungering desires after Christ, faith, love,
humility, meekness, self-denial, temperance, sincerity, righteousness, zeal for God's glory, and heav-
enly-mindedness? Have you found the beginnings of
the good work in your effectual calling and regeneration? And is the good work carrying towards perfection in your sanctification? Do you find sin more
and more mortified, the world more and more crucified, grace more and more strengthened? Can you
show any evidences of the indwelling of the Spirit?
Have you the teachings and quickenings of the
Spirit? Are you led by the Spirit out of the way of sin
into the paths of holiness and new obedience? Are
you brought near by the Spirit of God, and communion with Him and His ordinances? These are clear
evidences of the good work. Nothing is more worthy
of your inquiry than this: whether the good work of
grace is wrought in you by the Spirit.

USE 3. Here you have a powerful motive to
quicken your endeavors after this good work of
grace, if you are, for the present, without it. Nothing

is really more desirable than grace, which is so necessary, so excellent in itself, and withal so durable. If
you can attain true grace, you will get a jewel of the
greatest worth and use, and which will never be
taken away from you. What are all other things
which it is possible for any to gain in the world in
comparison with the gain of true grace? Will these
things abide? Can they prevent eternal misery?
Suppose you should get the best friends, most wise
and wealthy, most cordial and faithful unto you; the
best husbands or wives, most loving, sweet, and delightful; children full of sparkling wit and beauty
and most hopeful? Suppose you should get wealth in
abundance, silver, gold, jewels, houses, goods, lands,
and a large inheritance for your posterity? Suppose
you were lifted up to the highest seat of worldly
honor, advanced to the degree of nobility, yea,
kingly dignity, and with all these a confluence of all
sensual pleasures and a cup filled to the brim with
whatever delights any creatures could yield for you
to drink from every day. Yet the least dram of true
grace, accompanied with worldly poverty, disgrace,
and affliction is incomparably beyond all this in excellency; for besides the fact that these things are
not a suitable good for the soul, which is of higher
and larger capacity than to be filled up with them,
neither are they durable—if you had them you could
not keep them. And you would find more bitterness
in the loss of them than you ever found sweetness in
the enjoyment of them.

The kindness and love of friends may die; friends
themselves may die; and be sure you will die. Your
nearest relations may suddenly be snatched out of

your bosoms; your wealth may fly away swiftly like an eagle towards heaven; your honors may vanish away quickly like smoke in the air. You may lose all while you live; be sure you must leave all when you die. And think what a miserable condition you will be in at death if you have gained for yourselves only a portion in this life to show for all your days; for when your days are spent, your portion will be spent or left behind, and wholly lost to you forever. And alas! what must your soul do then? What must that live upon when it comes forth from your body? Where will your soul take itself? Alas! horror and woe, the regions of darkness, the company of devils, the treasures of God's wrath, and the most dreadful torments of hell must be the portion of your souls and bodies too at the resurrection if you live and die without this work of grace upon you.

But if you can attain unto true grace, it will advance you to the dignity of sons and daughters of God; it will join you in marriage to Christ, and bring you into the embraces of His love; it will repair God's image in you and restore you in some measure to man's primitive glory; it will rescue you out of the devil's chains and deliver you from the base servitude of sin; it will bring you under the beams of the light of God's countenance and fill you with most sweet peace of conscience and sometimes such soul-ravishing joy as words cannot utter; it will enrich your souls with the jewel of the greatest price here, and it will entitle you unto the treasures of glory, the undefiled, never-fading inheritance of heaven hereafter.

And besides the other excellencies of grace, this

is not the least: true grace can never be quite lost. Everything outside you may be lost, but grace within you can never be quite lost. Whatever has been wrought by you may be taken from you, but your grace cannot be lost. That which God has wrought in you will abide with you. Your estate may fail and your friends may fail, but your grace will never fail. When flesh and heart fail, your faith cannot quite fail and God will not fail.

And if your grace cannot be lost, be sure your souls are safe. They cannot be lost. Your happiness is safe; that cannot be touched. If you can get true grace, you shall never fall. Indeed, you may fall into affliction, but you shall not fall into sin. If you are not preserved from the evil worker, you shall be preserved from the evil work. If you fall into some acts of sin, you shall not fall into a course of sin. If you fall down, you shall not fall off. If you fall back, you shall not fall away. If you fall into the pit, you shall not fall into the bottomless pit. If your bodies fall into the grave, your souls shall not fall into hell. Devils may as soon be received into heaven as you, if gracious, can be cast into hell. If you get true grace, you cannot quite lose it. Therefore, you cannot miss glory. You shall as certainly have it as if you already had possession of it. God will as soon turn the angels out of heaven, He will as soon turn His own dear Son out of heaven, He will as soon leave that habitation Himself as shut you out of heaven at the end, if you have attained true grace. Who, then, would be without grace? Oh, then, prize grace; desire grace; seek grace; be ready to receive grace; and diligently improve all the means of grace for the attaining of this good work of grace within you.

USE 4. Oh, what a full breast of the sweetest consolation is this to all who are truly gracious! I think your hearts should be filled with comfort and leap for joy within you when you hear and are assured by the Word that the good work which God has begun in you in this day of grace He will perform until the day of Christ. What has been spoken by way of motive to sinners to incite them to get grace may be applied to you who are gracious by way of comfort. None in the world have reason to take comfort but you, and you have the most reason. I know that many ungracious persons who are still in the gall of bitterness and bond of iniquity have mirth and cheerfulness in their countenance and conversation, whatever their guilt and slavery, whatever their danger of eternal misery is, though they are already condemned and may be suddenly executed, and their ruin is likely to be inevitable because of their security.

On the contrary, I know that many truly gracious persons are full of fears and troubles, and walk up and down with a drooping countenance and a more sad heart, as if they were the persons who were designed unto destruction; as if they were miserable and should be miserable forever. I do not blame the jealousy of the gracious, lest they should be mistaken; but if upon a strict and impartial inquiry you can find evidences of the true work begun in you, although it is not yet brought to any great perfection, here you have a well and fountain opened (though some have endeavored in vain to stop it) of the greatest comfort and encouragement: God, who has begun the good work in you, will perform it. He will carry it on to perfection and carry you on by His power through faith unto salvation (1 Peter 1:5).

Some of you complain of affliction; but if you have grace you may well bear it; yea, and rejoice in it, because God is carrying on the good work of grace in you by it. Others complain of temptation, but if you have grace, though you shall be shaken, you shall not be quite overcome. And if the tempter does not presently depart from you yet God has promised that His grace shall be sufficient for you. Some complain of desertion, but if you have grace, though God hides His face, He will not remove His love. And remember that there is a bright side of the cloud of which you now only see the dark side; and ere long the shadows of this black night will be chased away by the bright beams of the light of God's countenance in the morning of His disclosure of Himself and love to you. Others complain of the strength of their corruptions, but if you have grace it will weaken them by degrees, and in the end will get a perfect victory over them. Some complain of the weakness of their graces, but you may be assured that your graces, weak as they are, shall never quite fail. God has engaged to carry on His own work in you which He has begun. Others complain that they have no evidences of any true grace, and they are afraid that they shall never hold out, that they shall fall away and turn into fearful apostates; but your graces may be true notwithstanding your doubts, and you may stand fast notwithstanding your fears. And let me tell you that hypocrites who are likely to prove apostates are usually very self-

confident. I fear those who are without such doubts
and fears more than you.

Happy are you that ever you were born if you are
indeed newborn. Happy are you in life; however
lowly and miserable you may be esteemed by the
world, none are so high born as those who are newborn; none are so beautiful as those who have God's
image; none are so adorned as those who have the
robes of Christ's righteousness; none are so en-
riched as those who have the riches of grace; none
have such company as those who have fellowship
with the Father and His Son, Jesus Christ; none have
such attendance as those who are attended by angels; none have such work as those who are employed in God's service; none have such liberty as
those who are freed from sin and Satan; none have
such peace as those who have peace of conscience;
none have such joy as those who have the joys of the
Holy Ghost; none have such safety as those who are
secured against total apostasy and eternal misery.

And this is your happiness if you are gracious in
life: you will be happy also at death. If your grace
does not free you from the stroke of death, it will
free you from the sting of death. If it does not free
you from the first death, it will free you from the
second death. Those who do not like your life will
wish they had your death. Balaam's wish is to be
found in the most ungracious wretch: "Let me die
the death of the righteous, and let my latter end be
like his."

But your happiness at the end of your lives is beyond the apprehension of the wicked; none can express with what ravishing comforts and joys some

gracious persons have departed from this life to their Father's house.

To conclude, you will be happy to eternity. If you are gracious, you will be glorious; if you are holy here, you will be happy hereafter. If God has begun the good work of grace, He will perform it until the day of Christ. You shall not lose your grace, and therefore you cannot miss your glory. Grace is glory begun, and you shall be transformed more and more into the image of God, from glory to glory, until you arrive unto perfection of glory. Ere long the Lord Jesus will appear, and then you shall appear with Him in glory; then you shall be presented before Him blameless and without spot; then you will lift up your heads with joy and your hearts will be filled with delight when you are raised out of your graves and caught up into the clouds to meet the Lord in the air, and there are welcomed into His presence with most ravishing looks and expressions of love, and He gives you full possession of His kingdoms. Then you will better know the excellency of this grace which you have now received when the fruit of it is brought forth, when the bud shall open in the flower, when the dawn has come to the day, when the promise has come to performance, when faith is turned into vision and hope into fruition, and all graces have arrived to perfection. Oh, the joys!

You only are happy who have this good work begun which the Lord will perform till the day of Christ. Oh, then, admire God's free grace in electing and calling you. Rejoice in Him and be very thankful, humble, and watchful, and walk worthy of

Him who has called you to His kingdom and glory.

There is one more use left, which is one of caution especially to young professors to take heed of apostasy and backsliding, which, without great care and heed, you may fall into, notwithstanding this doctrine. And therefore I have appended a letter for your caution, wherein you have a sad instance of a grievous backslider. Take heed from his falls.

Appendix 1

*A cautionary letter sent by an unknown author
to some youths belonging to the congregation
of Mr. Thomas Vincent*

Dear Friends,

Hearing of your Christian meetings, it came into my heart to write the following lines to you, which I hope will not discourage you, but rather caution you. Possibly you will be very inquisitive who wrote this letter, but I desire to be excused from giving my name. Assure yourselves that, however you may resent it, my intention is for your good.

It pleased God in my younger years to work a real change upon my heart, which was so visible to those about me that it could not be hidden from their notice, insomuch that I was a very wicked youth before. This sudden and great alteration filled the godly with joy, but the wicked made it a matter of laughter and derision. It pleased the Lord mightily to carry on this work a pretty while; my league with sin was quite broken off; my heart was (I think) united to the Lord Jesus Christ, and I was in love with Him, His Word, and His ordinances. Yea, all the ways of holiness were my delight. I found such sweetness in the ways of God that I even wonder that any could take delight in following any course of sin. I was, like Peter, confident that all the men on earth and

all the devils in hell could not draw me into a course
of sin again. I was constant in the performance of
secret duties, in which I spent no small time, even
all I could spare from my master's business, and
then had great purposes and resolution that if the
Lord spared me till I could command my own time I
would spend much more than I had spent in religious duties.

Briefly, the hardest of duties and the heaviest
burdens seemed light to me then. The Lord had
given me great conquests over my corruptions, so
that I was like in heaven while on earth. But, alas!
My dear friends, this did not last more than a year
and a half or thereabouts. Being ignorant of Satan's
temptations and my own heart's deceitfulness and
baseness, I dreamed not of any other thing but what
I had found. But here I am hindered awhile in writ-
ing by a flood of tears and sorrow, to think how
strangely my condition is altered, so that I can but
just call to mind the days of old and the years of the
right hand of the Most High.

Now, having given you a short account of my
most joyful times, of my halcyon days, which are almost a score of years past with me (yet I hope will
always be present with you, God grant, ye may not
sin them away and taste of my miseries), I shall give
you a few lines of my sad and wretched times since,
together with the occasion of my troubles.

When the Lord had dealt thus graciously with
me, the Quakers' opinion being newly risen up, I
was often talking with them, and thereby put upon
reading disputes to defend myself against them, and
also was very eager to know all opinions, which stole

so fast upon me that it swallowed up most that time
which I should have spent reading more profitable
things, or in meditation, heart examination, and
prayer.

I was then over-conceited of my wit, very proud of
my gifts, apt to undervalue all who had not the same.
Yea, doubtless, pride was the chief sin, for which the
Lord left me to commit so many evils. By little and
little my communion with God abated, I fell into
some smaller sins, and duties were first slightly performed and then totally neglected for a consider-
able time. Oh, how like a beast I laid down and rose
again without seeking the Lord! I suppose the whole
earth's riches would not formerly have made me
omit one praying time, but now I might be num-
bered among the heathens, and those who do not
call upon God.

After this, I deserted (as much as I could) all
good company; sin now came in by whole troops:
any frothy persons were my companions. I then exceeded due bounds in eating, drinking and sleeping. I fell to gaming, stealing, lying, was full of un-
chaste desires, and hardly refrained from commit-
ting the sin of uncleanness. Conscience was mostly
wasted, the tenderness being gone. Could I give a
catalogue of the sins I have been left to commit, it
would strain your charity to think I ever had grace.

I was many times under dreadful apprehensions
what would be the issue of my wicked life and apostasy. The Lord then followed me with one scourge
after another. I was hedged up so that I have been
forced to submit to the Lord and have been under
great humblings. But a strong temptation, when the

Lord's mercies have been removed, has overcome
me again, and in the same manner several times.
And now I can set my seal to that truth in Proverbs
14:14: "The backslider in heart shall be filled with
his own ways." Very sad is that man or woman's state
whom the Lord punishes by allowing sin to rule
over them. And how can I expect that such a wretch
as I should be the instrument to do you the least
good, except that I think the Lord can, by His great
wisdom, do good by evil instruments; therefore it
may be of some use to some of you.

For, I thought, when I heard of your forwardness,
I foresaw, as it were, one ready to decline in his fervor, another fainting and growing weary of God's
ways: one is ready to venture upon sin, another begins to set up in the world and is swallowed up with
business, cares of family, fears of poverty, breakings
out into passions when their affairs do not have the
desired success, discontent, and then growing re-
miss in closet and family duties, first neglecting one
duty, then at last religion is almost laid aside. Then
they fall into loose and drinking company, and neglect their general and particular callings.

Oh, beware, dear youths, for the Lord's sake and
for your own sakes. The least that can come of such
things is great dishonor to God and great trouble to
you, such as you may never get off while you live. You
will be pierced through with many sorrows. If there
is no peace to the wicked, surely then the godly must
not have peace in wickedness. You will still be ques-
tioning and fearing (as I do this day) whether the
work was true, and these sins like the spots of God's
children.

Then, I pray you, accept a few words of advice and do not slight them, though commonly known.

1. Beware of pride at all times, whether bodily or spiritual, or pride regarding gifts and graces. Oh, labor much (if ever you will be a persevering Christian) against this sin! I know the devil will be very busy puffing you up with good conceits of your own duties. Be not content with gifts; labor chiefly to grow in grace, and in particular the grace of humility (Isaiah 57:15).

2. Beware of disputings. If you are addicted to them, I truly think the devil will furnish you with arguments and new notions, with the design that they shall eat out the power of godliness.

3. Beware of coveting many books. Books are good helps if rightly used. Study well those truths that are preached weekly.

4. Fear every motion to neglect a known duty or to commit a known sin. Do not grieve the blessed Comforter.

5. Beware of taking the utmost liberty you might take, if you were sure your hearts would crave no more in eating, drinking, sleeping, apparel, or recreations.

6. Make great conscience to discharge relative duties to parents, masters, and the like. Those who wrong masters are as real thieves as those who steal goods or money. Read over the promises and covenants you made with your masters in your indentures.

7. Take heed what company you associate with. Go with fear into a woman's company; set a watch upon your heart and eyes.

8. Avoid all unmerciful severity to your bodies by too frequent or overlong fasting, or the like; for the devil is very subtle with young people here. Doubtless he puts them upon it to the end that he may tire them out and make God's ways burdensome to them.

9. Beware of scornful thoughts towards those who are without much of the world's goods; have bowels of pity and love towards them.

10. Be careful to praise God for mercy. This duty I was much lacking in, though I was loaded with mercies.

11. Beware of self-confidence; lean only on Christ.

12. Do not go to a tavern or alehouse except with great fear and watchfulness. Do not go at all but upon necessary occasions. Take heed of idleness; take heed of tale-bearing.

I have done now. I only desire your joint prayers for me that the Lord would heal my broken bones, and that He will prevent your falling into sin (Matthew 18:19–20).

Appendix 2

A Return of Thanks to the Author
of the Previous Letter

Sir,

I believe you will wonder a little to see your letter (written and sent so privately unto my dear youths) come forth into public view without your knowledge. I hope you will take it as a sufficient excuse for me, who has taken confidence to do it, that, not knowing your person or place of abode, nor any way as to how I might come to you or send something to you, I was not in a capacity to ask your permission, as I would have done with the return of many thanks for your seasonable caution and advice which you have given unto young professors.

I suppose that these lines will come into your hands without the notice of any; they are accompanied with my prayers for your perfect recovery, and, as you desire, that God would heal your broken bones, restore to you the joy of His salvation, and establish you for the future with His free Spirit. You have, I fear, been a rock of offense— not like our Savior, but like Peter when he fell—unto those who have been acquainted with your profession and with your fall. If by the publishing of your case you prove a rock above water to keep some young ones from shipwreck, I hope you will not be offended with this publication. The flood of tears you speak of remembering your foolish backsliding and departure from God, together with the honest design of your letter, give me ground to hope the best concerning your estate.

I am loath to rake into those wounds which seem to be bleeding, and to answer kind and seasonable admonitions with sharp reproofs. Your free and ingenious confessions evidently demonstrate that you have a faithful Reprover in your own bosom, and if you can make such acknowledgments unto men for their caution, I do not doubt that you have often made these acknowledgments unto God in order to your own remission. I would gladly have read a line or two in your paper of your recovery, but by the broken bones you complain of in the close you seem to be down still. I will not say "down" in regard of sin (I hope you have been long ago awakened from your gross neglects of God and duty, and have broken off your loose company and conversation), but in regard of sorrow and a disconsolate spirit. It may be you are still without that liveliness and vigor which you had at first.

Truly, I don't wonder at your broken bones, after you have ventured upon such breaches of God's laws. I don't wonder at God's frowns after such provocations, and that God should hide Himself from you when you have run away from Him. I don't wonder that God withdraws His Spirit from you a long time, in regard of its witnessing, comforting, and quickening operation. I don't wonder when you have not only grieved, but quenched and driven away the Spirit by your great backslidings. Yet one

Scripture I would recommend to you for your encouragement and consolation, which possibly you have not taken such notice of, and that is Hosea 11:7–9: "My people are bent to backsliding from Me, though they called them to the Most High, none at all would exalt Him. How shall I give thee up, Ephraim! How shall I deliver thee, Israel! How shall I make thee as Admah! How shall I set thee as Zeboim! Mine heart is turned within Me, My repentings are kindled together. I will not execute the fierceness of Mine anger; I will not return to destroy Ephraim. For I am God and not man."

Your sin has not only been backsliding (which is a high affront and indignity offered unto God, casting a great slur upon Him and His ways, as if upon trial of Him and the creature, the ways of holiness and the ways of sin, the latter were the better and more eligible: this has been the language of your courses), but you have been bent to backsliding. The devil has hampered and held you in his snares when you have fallen, and, when you have endeavored to rise, he has pulled you down again by his cords. Your heart has been bent to revolt from God, which you intimate in your letter. It is likely that you have often been called to return to the Most High by His messengers and ministers, but still you have persisted in dishonoring God instead of exalting Him. This has been your carriage towards God, as it was the carriage of Israel of old.

But see the carriage of God towards such backsliders. What is that? Is it fury, indignation, and vengeance? What does God say to such a people? Is it, "How shall I not give you up to ruins? How shall I

not deliver you to destruction? How shall I not con-
sume you with the fire of My anger, as I consumed
Admah and Zeboim, with Sodom and Gomorrah of
old, by fire and brimstone from heaven?"

Read and tremble! Consider and wonder! God's
language is quite contrary to this: "How shall I give
thee up, Ephraim? How shall I deliver thee, Israel?
How shall I make thee as Admah? And set thee as
Zeboim?" One would have thought that God's heart
and hand too would have been turned against
Ephraim, backsliding and provoking Ephraim, and
that His anger would not only have been kindled
against Ephraim, but blown up by such provocations
into such a flame as would have proved unquenchable! But wonder and weep that you have provoked
such a gracious God who is so ready to be reconciled.

God's heart is turned within Him towards
Ephraim, and His repentings are kindled together.
He promises that He will not execute the fierceness
of His anger in the destruction of Ephraim. And the
reason for all is not any motive from Ephraim, but
all is from Himself: "For I am God and not man."
What man would have borne what God has borne?
Who would have been so affronted and not avenged
himself if it lay in the power of his hand to do so?
But God has not only forborne to punish, but He is
also ready to forgive; and that is because He is God
and not man. His mercies are infinitely beyond the
mercies of men. Our bowels are marble in comparison with God's most tender compassions. He blots
out transgressions for His name's sake; and He has
promised to heal backslidings (Hosea 14:4). Read

especially Jeremiah 3, and be encouraged to return
unto, and for the future to follow, the Lord fully.
Take the counsel which Christ gave unto the
backsliding church of Ephesus after she had left her
first love. Revelation 2:4–5: "Remember whence thou
art fallen, and repent and do thy first works." And
the counsel which He gave to the languishing
church of Sardis in Revelation 3:2: "Be watchful, and
strengthen the things which remain that are ready
to die."

Had I time and room, and were more exactly acquainted with the present state of your soul, I would
further attempt to give you some suitable advice out
of the Word of God by way of requital for your great
care and kindness toward our youths. In the meantime, let these few acknowledgments be accepted
from a real well-wisher to your soul,

Thomas Vincent

Appendix 3

*Cautionary motives and directions unto youths
professing religion, to keep them from
apostasy and backsliding*

You have heard that the good work which God
has begun in the day of grace He will perform
until the day of Christ. Yet, lest any should
abuse this doctrine, and turn the grace of God into
wantonness; lest any should, by presuming that the
good work has begun in them, and thence conclud-
ing that they shall never fall away, presume also to
indulge themselves in sin, and hence take occasion
to give way unto licentiousness; therefore I shall add
a serious caution unto all, especially to young professors.

In 1 Corinthians 10, and at the beginning of the
chapter, the Apostle spreads before the Corinthians
some examples from Scripture of the falls of the
children of Israel in the wilderness—their falling
into sin and falling into mischief and ruin thereby.
In verse 11 he tells them that all those things hap-
pened unto them for examples, and were written for
their admonition. And therefore he gives caution to
them in verse 12: "Wherefore let him that thinketh
he standeth take heed lest he fall."

In like manner I have spread before you a letter
directed to you from one who, when he was a young

apprentice, as many of you are, was wrought upon, as you have been. He tells you what his attainments and enjoyments were, so that he then was a high and forward professor; but withal he acknowledges that in a short time he declined, fell into sin, and became a fearful backslider. And as he has written it, so I have published it for your admonition that I might give you the Apostle's caution: "Let him that thinketh he standeth take heed lest he fall."

Motives to Keep from Apostasy and Backsliding
1. Some have and may fall, and apostasize from the ways of God, who have made a high profession of religion, attained great illumination, gifts, and tastes of spiritual things. These may have been thought by others, and themselves too, to have stood as surely as any. Therefore, all who think they stand, especially you who are young professors, should take heed lest you fall. The Apostle tells Timothy (2 Timothy 4:10) that Demas had forsaken him, having loved this present world. And before that (1 Timothy 1:19–20) he tells of Hymenaeus and Alexander, who had put away a good conscience and made shipwreck of the faith, and who had learned to blaspheme. The Apostle Peter speaks in 2 Peter 2:20–22 of some who had escaped the pollutions of the world through the knowledge of Christ, who now were entangled again and overcome, and that this was according to the old proverb: "The dog is turned to his own vomit again, and the sow that was washed unto her wallowing in the mire." Our Savior tells us in His explication of the Parable of the Sower (Matthew 13:20–21) that he who received the

Word in stony places is he who hears the Word and receives it with joy; yet not having any root in himself, he only endures for awhile, for when tribulation arises because of the Word, by and by he is offended. Indeed, such as have true grace can never totally fall, as has been proven, but many may have that which is like true grace and may fall totally from it. They may lose that which they seem to have.

2. Apostasy is a very high God-provoking sin. Hebrews 10:38: "If any man draw back, My soul shall have no pleasure in him." This drawing back is not to be understood of the backslidings of God's children, but of the apostasy of hypocrites, such a drawing back as is unto perdition (verse 39). God's soul has no pleasure in them, that is, He is highly displeased with them. Apostates, in effect, say that upon trial they have found the devil to be a better master than Christ, and the ways of sin and wickedness, though they lead to death and hell, to be more eligible than the ways of God and holiness, though they lead to life and glory.

3. Besides the sin of apostasy itself, which is so heinous, such as are guilty of it usually grow worse than they were before in all kinds of licentious conduct. Matthew 12:43–45: "When the unclean spirit is gone out of a man, and returneth again, he taketh seven other spirits more wicked than himself, and they enter in and dwell there, and the last estate of that man is worse than the first." Apostates are the firstborn children of the devil, and the lusts of their father they will do. He dwells in them and rules over them, and they are ready at his motion for any wickedness. Besides uncleanness, debauchery, mis-

chief, villany, oaths, and blasphemy, such persons usually have the most desperate enmity against God and godliness, and of all others prove the greatest persecutors of the saints.

Yea, apostates are upon the threshold of the sin against the Holy Ghost, and many of them step over into it, and then there is no returning for them and renewing them unto repentance. There is no sacrifice for their sin, no remission attainable by them, so that their damnation is certain and the fiery indignation unavoidable which shall devour them.

I don't say that all apostates fall into the unpardonable sin; yet I had almost said that all apostates fall so as never to rise again in the event and issue; if their sins are not unpardonable, they prove almost always unpardonable. Jude 12 compares some to trees whose fruit withers, without fruit, twice dead, and plucked up by the roots. Such are apostates, whose seeming fruit withering, and whose seeming life being lost, are twice dead; they are so plucked up by the roots that they can never receive life again. I don't remember ever hearing or reading of an apostate who has been converted.

4. And therefore apostasy almost always ends in perdition. Hebrews 10:39: "We are not of them that draw back to perdition." Such bring upon themselves destruction and swift destruction. Their judgment lingers not and their damnation slumbers not (2 Peter 2:1, 3). God quickly awakens them to the vengeance which He has appointed for them. They also bring upon themselves most dreadful destruction: besides the torture of the body, which such must undergo in the flames of hell, they will surpass

others in the anguish and horror of their minds. None will have such furious reflections and horrible lashes of conscience as apostates, when they perceive what happiness they fell from when they fell from the ways of holiness, and what misery they fell into when they fell into sin. Beware, then, you who profess religion now in your younger years, that you do not prove to be apostates when you are elder, and thereby verify that profane proverb, "young saints and old devils." Do not so bring upon yourselves such aggravated guilt, and draw down such an unsupportable weight of wrath as will sink you so low in hell.

5. If you have the good work of grace begun in you, and if God has engaged to perform it and keep you so that you shall never fall away, yet it is by motives considered and means made use of that He does it. If you should live in neglect of these means, you cannot expect to be kept by God from total apostasy. And if you presume upon God's keeping you in the neglect of the means which He has appointed for your establishment, it is a great sign of your hypocrisy, and the unsoundness of the grace which you profess to have.

6. Though God will not allow you totally to fall from grace if the good work is in truth begun in you, yet, without great heed, you may fall into great decay of grace; your graces may languish and so be ready to die (Revelation 3:2). You may fall into swooning fits and a lethargic distemper so that there shall appear little evidence of life in you, either to yourselves or to others. You may, instead of the sweet meltings for sin which you have, grow in-

sensible and contract a great stupidity and hardness of heart; instead of your pliableness and readiness to spiritual duties, you may contract a listlessness and indisposition; instead of your humility and self-loathing, you may grow very proud and self-conceited; instead of your meek and gentle temper, you may grow peevish and passionate; instead of your uprightness of heart, and your single eye to God's glory, you may spoil most of your duties with hypocrisy; instead of self-denial and temperance, you may indulge yourself and grow licentious in a great measure. You may lose much of your contentment and patience, and the fear of God which you now have. Your hungering desire after Christ may be abated; your now strong faith may become feeble; your flames of love may be quenched; the flame quite gone, and only some coals or sparks remain imperceivable under the ashes; your hopes of heaven may be lost, as to the liveliness and delightful working of them. Therefore, beware lest you fall.

7. If you do not fall totally from grace, yet, without heed, you may fall foully into sin. You have read in Scripture of some gross sins with which some saints have been overtaken: Noah's drunkenness, Lot's incest, David's murder and adultery, Job's and Jeremiah's cursing their birthday, Jonah's passionate speeches to God for sparing Nineveh, Peter's denial of his Master, and so on. And if you do not look well to yourselves, you also (though you have true grace) may fall into some foul sins to the dishonor of God and your profession, to the wounding of Christ and your conscience, to the grieving of the Spirit and God's people, to the eclipsing of the light

of God's countenance, to the interrupting of all sensible communion with God, to the darkening of your evidence for heaven, to the losing of all spiritual joy and peace, to provoking God to scourge you severely in your bodies, estates, names and friends, and to deliver you to Satan and the tyrannizing power of lust.

You may fall so as hereby to be filled not only with fears, but with horrors; and not only to faint through doubt of your estates, but also to sink through an almost utter despair of mercy. You may sin so as not only to lose God's smiles, but also to gain His frowns, and, having lost all evidences for heaven, you may be brought even to the brink of hell in your own apprehension. Sad and doleful is the condition of some backsliding children of God through their falls, which should be a warning to others to take heed of the like.

8. Though you are truly gracious, yet you are in danger of falling, and in great danger without great heed; partly through the temptations of Satan, that implacable, busy, watchful, invisible, false, deceitful enemy who sometimes will furiously assault and, like a roaring lion, fall upon you to make a prey of you and devour you; but most commonly will use cunning insinuations with you suitable to your natural dispositions and inclinations. By his secret snares he will endeavor to entangle you before you are aware. You are partly in danger of falling through the world, which sometimes will smile upon you to allure you, at other times will frown upon you to frighten you. Sometimes it will promise its good things to draw you, and at other times will

threaten its evil things to drive you into sin. But the chief danger of all which you are in of falling is from yourselves, from your own deceitful hearts and the remainder of unmortified, corrupt flesh within you. Hereby you may be betrayed, and the flesh, joining with the world and the devil, may hurry you into the commission of such sins which you now think you would not commit for all the world's riches, and if all the imperial diadems of the earth were thrown down at your feet.

9. You may be kept from falling if you look well to your standing. Whatever your danger is, God can keep you and hold up your goings in His paths so that your footsteps do not slip. Jude 24: "To Him that is able to keep you from falling, and to present you faultless before the presence of His glory, with exceeding joy." Yea, He has promised to keep you, and has engaged His faithfulness to do it in your applying yourselves to Him, making use of the means which He has appointed for your upholding and establishment. 2 Thessalonians 3:3: "But the Lord is faithful who shall establish you, and keep you from evil."

And I shall add that it is more easy (besides the honor brought hereby unto God, and the inexpressible benefit and comfort to yourselves) to stand, not to fall and then to arise and get up when you are fallen. It is no easy thing to recover out of a backsliding state. Such as backslide very much do not usually or easily or presently recover themselves. And many never recover themselves fully as long as they live. As they lose some measures of grace here, so they are likely to miss those degrees of glory which otherwise they would have attained unto.

Directions to Keep from Apostasy and Backsliding
     1. Look to it that the good work is indeed begun
in your hearts, that you have grace of the right kind.
If you should prove, notwithstanding all your profession, unsound in the main points, rotten at the
core, false-hearted hypocrites, you are in great danger of total apostasy, against which you have no
promise from God for your security. The profession
of hypocrites is built upon a sandy foundation,
which the wind of affliction and storms of persecution will overturn. It is only true grace that is of an
establishing nature. Hebrews 13:9: "It is a good
thing that the heart be established with grace." Only
the truly gracious are built upon the rock of ages
where they are safe; and however they may be shaken
by troubles and temptations, yet they shall never be
utterly cast down and quite overturned.
     2. Be very humble. Proverbs 16:18: "Pride goeth
before destruction, and a haughty spirit before a
fall." Tall cedars are overthrown with the wind when
humble and low shrubs are hardly touched by its
blasts. And when God resists the proud and allows
them to be thrown down, He gives grace to the lowly
and strengthens them to stand.
     3. Stand not in your own strength. None have
fallen more foully than the presumptuous self-con-
fident; labor for a fear and jealousy of yourselves.
Romans 11:20: "Be not high-minded, but fear." Let
your confidence and strength be in the Lord. 2 Timothy 2:1: "Be strong in the grace which is in Christ
Jesus." Have recourse to Him for grace to help in

every need and under every assault and temptation which you have to sin. Christ is able to give aid; it is His office to give aid, and He is ready to do so. He pities you when you are tempted and is touched with the feelings of your infirmities (Hebrews 4:15); He has invited you to come unto Him (verse 16), and has promised that He will bruise Satan under your feet shortly (Romans 16:20). In the meantime, His grace shall be sufficient for you (2 Corinthians 12:9).

4. Study and apply the promises of perseverance and preservation from sin: that God will confirm you to the end (1 Corinthians 1:8), that He will hold you in His hand, from whence none shall pluck you (John 10:29), that He will keep you from departing from Him (Jeremiah 32:40), that He will preserve you from every evil work, and that unto His heavenly kingdom (2 Timothy 4:18). The whole Scripture is useful in this way. David hid God's Word in his heart as a preservative against sin (Psalm 119:11).

But the promises are more especially useful, being of such a cleansing and establishing virtue, especially these and similar promises whereby God has obliged and engaged Himself to establish His people from falls. Therefore, be conversant with the Word, and receive it not only in the light of it, but also in the love of it, whereby you will be kept from falling into either damnable error or scandalous sin.

5. Avoid vain janglings, and an itch to dispute with such as are of contrary opinions. Take heed how you have any conversation with those who are tainted in their judgments, or at least of wrangling disputes with them; for, besides your hazard, espe-

cially while you are young and inexperienced, of being seduced by them, you will be in danger of declining in the vigor of your spirits and the fervor of your love to God. The author of the cautionary letter has told you of his sad experience, how his fall began upon his engaging in disputes with the Quakers. Acquaint yourselves well with the principles of religion which you have in your catechisms, and see how they are proven by the Scriptures. Hold fast those truths, and turn away from those that endeavor to steal them away and rob you of them.

6. Take heed of sensuality and indulging the flesh. In your youth, you may be most prone to this; temptations may be pressing and inclinations strong, but you must exercise yourselves in self-denial and keep a hard hand over your rebellious flesh. You must, if need be, keep under your body; be sure to bring your sensual appetites and desires into subjection to your reason regulated by the Word. If those desires get loose and gain the mastery, think what precipices of sin you are likely to fall into.

7. Beware of wordly-mindedness, so that you are not swallowed up with worldly business and encumbered with the affairs of this life. I am sure this will cause a great decay in the power of godliness. If the world, by reason of your callings, has most of your time, take heed that it has not all; reserve some time every day for religious exercises, and let them have most of your hearts. Take heed of inordinate cares, fears, and griefs about worldly things on one side, and inordinate love, desires, and delights on the other side. Endeavor to get the world crucified to you, and your hearts crucified to it. Make use of the

cross of Christ in order hereunto, and take frequent view of the transcendent glory and happiness of the other world, which will disgrace the world in your esteem.

8. Stand continually upon your watch. Beware of sin in the beginning of it; do not so much as entertain sin in your minds with any pleasing, delightful thoughts; refrain from secret sins, otherwise your feet will slide up before you are aware. Take heed of the least degree of apostasy; observe your hearts when they begin to go off from God, and endeavor with all speed to recover and rise again when you feel yourselves beginning to fall.

9. Labor after further growth in grace every day. Give all diligence to make some additions daily to your graces; and hereby you will both make your calling and election sure. And if you do these things you shall never fall (2 Peter 1:10). While grace is growing, it cannot be declining; and therefore you cannot fall.

10. Prize and improve the means of grace: the Word and sacraments, and all strengthening ordinances. Look to God's institution of them as the means of establishment, and seek after God's preference in them. Wait for the breathings of His Spirit, and cherish the Spirit's influences both of grace and of comfort, which are of great efficacy to keep you from falling.

11. Make the most fruitful, experienced, established, zealous, and warm-hearted Christians your most intimate companions. Forsake not only the company of the loose and profane, but also of such as have a form of godliness, but deny the power

thereof, as is the Apostle's advice in 2 Timothy 3:5: "From such turn away." Associate yourselves as much as you can with those who fear the Lord. Labor to improve yourself by their company. Great encouragement and help you may attain by the converse of lively Christians.

12. Set God always before your eyes as David did, and withal tells us that because God was at his right hand he should not be moved (Psalm 16:8). Temptations to sin will little move you when you actually look to and consider God's eye upon you. You will easily answer and repel temptations. "How can I do this wickedness and sin against God?"

13. Labor for a strong and fervent love to God. Many waters cannot quench the fire of this love. While your hearts are mounting upwards in this flame unto God, you are not in such danger of falling down and giving ear unto temptations which would draw you into sin. Labor to dwell in the love of God and the love of one another. Hereby you will dwell in God and God in you (1 John 4:16). And while you dwell in God, you cannot fall from Him.

14. Be much in secret conversation with God in meditation, contemplation, short and secret prayers. Go often to your knees when you are alone, and there bewail sin and pray for the mortification of your special corruptions. Secret duties seriously, diligently, and constantly performed are both an evidence of sincerity and a great preservative against apostasy.

15. Lastly, and chiefly, labor for much of the grace of faith and put it forth into daily exercise. 2 Corinthians 1:24: "By faith ye stand." If you would

resist the devil you must be steadfast in faith (1 Peter 5:8–9). If you would quench his fiery darts you must get on and hold up the shield of faith (Ephesians 6:16). If you would be kept by the power of God it must be through faith unto salvation (1 Peter 1:5). Such as draw back unto perdition, it is through unbelief. Such as hold out, it is through faith to the saving of their souls (Hebrews 10:39).

I shall close my discourse with two Scriptures. 1 Corinthians 16:13: "Watch ye, stand fast in the faith, quit ye like men, be strong." And 1 Corinthians 15:58: "Therefore, my beloved brethren, be steadfast and unmovable, always abounding in the work of the Lord. Forasmuch as ye know that your labor is not in vain in the Lord."

Christic the Best Husband

Inviting young women to Christ

Hearken (O daughter), and consider, and incline thine ear; forget also thine own people, and thy father's house; so shall the King greatly desire thy beauty; for he is thy Lord, and worship thou him."

Psalm 45:10–11

This psalm is called a song of loves, the most high, pure, and spiritual, the most dear, sweet, and delightful loves, namely those loves which are between Christ the Beloved and His Church, which is His spouse. Here is set forth, first, the Lord Jesus Christ in His majesty, power, and divinity, His truth, meekness, and equity; and then the spouse is set forth in regard of her ornaments, companions, attendants, and posterity. And both are set forth in regard of their loveliness and beauty. After a description is given of Christ, an invitation is made to His espousals, and that of the children of men, called by the name of "daughter." Therefore it is particularly applicable unto the daughters of men, yet not so as excluding the sons of men as any more than when God speaks unto the sons of men He excludes the daughters. I shall now speak unto the words, and from hence observe this doctrine, as comprehensive as I can make it.

94

DOCTRINE: The Lord Jesus Christ, the King of glory, invites all the children of men, particularly the daughters of men, to be His spouse. He is exceedingly desirous of their beauty who, forgetting their people and their father's house, hearken, consider, and incline to His invitation, and join themselves to Him in this relationship.

In handling this point, I shall speak concerning Christ's espousing Himself unto the children of men; show that Christ invites all the children of men, and particularly the daughters of men, to be His spouse; that such who would be espoused unto Jesus Christ must hearken, consider, and incline to His invitation, and forget their own people and father's house; that such as are espoused unto Jesus Christ are very beautiful; that Jesus Christ greatly desires the beauty of such as are espoused unto Him; and lastly make some application.

1. Christ espouses and betroths people unto Himself in this world. The public solemnization of the marriage is reserved until the last day when His spouse shall be brought to Him in white robes and raiment of perfect righteousness, more rich and curious than any needlework. The marriage feast will be held in His Father's house in heaven, where they shall be received into the nearest and closest embraces of His love. The espousal between them and the marriage knot is tied here. There are four things chiefly included in Christ's espousal with the children of men: mutual choice, mutual affection, mutual union, and mutual obligation.

Mutual Choice: Besides the eternal choice which is not only in Christ as Mediator, but also by Christ as the eternal Son of God, Christ in time actually chooses some of the children of men, passing by others, without the least respect to any worthiness or desirable qualification in them. He does so freely, of His mere grace, to make them His spouse, and to bring them into the marriage covenant and relation to Himself. And herein Christ begins: He chooses them first, as He tells His disciples in John 15:16: "Ye have not chosen Me, but I have chosen you." And then they make choice of Him above all to take Him for their Lord and Husband. Christ finds them deformed, defiled, enslaved, poor, miserable, wretched, very despicable, and loathsome because of sin. And He makes choice of them not because they have any beauty or suitable qualifications for this match, but that He may put His beauty and comeliness upon them, and endow them with such qualifications as may make them fit for His embraces. But in their making choice of Christ, they are drawn to Him by the most attractive and powerful motives of the transcendent beauty and superlative excellency which they see in Him beyond all persons and things in the world.

Mutual Affection: In this espousal there is mutual affection; this accompanies the choice. On Christ's part, at first He bears a love of benevolence unto those whom He espouses, and desires the nearest union and conjunction with them, and therefore makes suit to them for their love. On their part, their hearts are drawn forth in desires after Christ. "None but Christ, none but Christ!" is the language of their hearts when they are made thoroughly sensible of their need of Him. And however His dowry at first is most desired, yet afterwards, as they get more acquainted, they are most taken with His person.

Mutual Union: In this espousal there is mutual union, and herein most properly does the espousal lie. In this union Christ and souls are contracted, and the knot is tied so tightly that no power can untie it. This union is by the Spirit on Christ's part, and by faith on the soul's part; by the Spirit Christ lays hold of them, and by faith they lay hold of Christ; by the Spirit Christ draws and knits them to Himself, and by faith they come and join themselves to Him, and so the match is made. Christ becomes theirs: His person, His portion, and all His benefits are theirs. And they become Christ's: their persons, their hearts, and all that they have is resigned up to Him.

Mutual Obligation: In this espousal there is mutual obligation. Christ obliges Himself to them to love them and never leave them, to protect, to provide for them, to live with them here, and at length to take them to live with Him forever. And they engage themselves to Him to be loving, loyal, faithful, obedient, and with full purpose of heart to stick close to Him as long as they live. This is implied in the espousal itself.

2. Christ invites all the children of men, and particularly the daughters of men, to be His spouse; this is that which they are invited to in the text. It is upon this account that Christ sends His ministers to be His ambassadors, to whom He gives commission in His name to call the children of men unto this most near and sweet relationship; they represent His

person, and are to invite and woo in His name so
that people would come and join themselves unto
Him. The Apostle Paul tells the Corinthians how
successful His embassage was among them in 2 Corinthians 11:2: "I have espoused you unto one husband, that I may present you as a chaste virgin unto
Christ." And when any ministers are instrumental in
the conversion of any, they espouse them to Christ.
In conversion sinners are divorced from sin and are
married unto the Lord Jesus.

The Lord, by His Word in the mouth of His ministers, makes a general invitation unto all the children of men, and particularly all the daughters of
men are invited to be Christ's spouse: "Hearken, O
daughter, and consider, incline thine ear." Such as
are older are invited, but especially those who are
younger, whether married or unmarried, of higher
degree or meanest quality, even the poorest servants
are as welcome to be Christ's spouse as those who
are rich. He does not regard the rich more than the
poor. He chose a mean virgin, espoused to a carpen-
ter, to be His mother. And He chooses and calls all
such, and those which are lower than such, to be
His spouse.

3. Such as would be espoused unto Jesus Christ
must hearken, consider and incline to His invitation, and forget their people and father's house.

Such as would be espoused unto Christ must hearken.
"Hearken, O daughter." Some, yea, most of the children of men shut their eyes as fast as they can
against the light of the Word, and they shut their
ears as fast as they can against the calls of the Word.
They are like the deaf adder that will not hearken to

the voice of the charmer, though he charms never so wisely. So these will not hearken to the invitations of Christ by His ministers, let them invite never so pathetically. It was by the ear that the temptation to sin was received at first by man when he departed from God, and it is by the ear that the invitation to be Christ's spouse is first received, whereby any are restored unto God's favor. The ear must first be opened to receive Christ's invitation before the heart will be opened to receive Jesus Christ in this conjugal relation. Isaiah 55:3: "Hear, and thy soul shall live."

Such as would be espoused unto Christ must not only hearken, but consider Christ's invitation: "Hearken, O daughter, and consider." It is not a slight or bare hearing of Christ's invitation which will make up the match between Christ and the soul, but there must be a considering, a pondering of it in the mind. There must be a considering of the offer itself, what it is, the reality of the thing, the necessity of the thing, that attainableness of it, the greatness of it, the freeness of it, the sweetness of it, the advantage of it, the difference between Christ's invitations and the devil's temptations, or any of the world's offers. And by such considering and weighing one against the other, the soul will come to understand, and be fully persuaded, that Christ's invitations are most reasonable and eligible.

Such as would be espoused unto Christ must incline unto Christ's invitation: "Hearken, O daughter, and consider, incline thine ear." I suppose by the inclining of the ear is not meant the hearkening just before; but it includes the inclining of the heart to accept

Christ's invitation. There must be a consent of the will and a ready compliance with Christ's motion, a closing of the heart with it. This shows itself when the soul is not only sued to accept Christ, but when it puts forth desires after Christ and sues to Him that it may be accepted into this relationship. David inclined to the invitation for the Lord to seek His face in Psalm 27:8: "When Thou saidest, 'Seek ye My face,' my heart said unto Thee, 'Thy face, Lord, will I seek.' " So the childen of men incline to Christ's invitations to be His spouse when their hearts say, "Lord, let us be Thy spouse, and be Thou our beloved."

Such as would be espoused unto Jesus Christ must forget their people and father's house: "Hearken, O daughter, and consider, forget thy own people and thy father's house." Not as if by espousing themselves unto Christ they are ready to cast off all affections for natural relations, but they must so forget all relations so as to be ready to forgo all their favor when it stands in competition with Christ. They must be ready to displease anyone rather than to displease Christ; to suffer the loss of anything rather than to lose His favors. They must forget their own people and father's house; that is, they must forget all the evil customs which they have learned in their father's house, and forsake the vain conversation received by tradition from their fathers, from which Christ has redeemed them (1 Peter 1:18). Some think the words literally are an invitation of Pharaoh's daughter to come out of Egypt and forget her people and father's house there that she might be espoused to King Solomon. And so hereby the

Lord, in calling upon people to be espoused to Him, would have them come forth from the Egypt of sin and forget and forsake all their former sinful courses and conversation. And truly such as are in Egyptian bondage to sin have a father, the devil, and their companions in sin may be called their own people. These they must forget and forsake and come out from among—if not in regard of place, at least in regard of course, if they would be espoused unto the Lord Jesus.

4. Such as are espoused unto the Lord Jesus are very beautiful. I don't mean in regard of their bodies; they may have less external comeliness than others, and yet, in regard of their bodies (however mean and vile, however crooked and decrepit some of them may now be), even their bodies shall be formed and fashioned into an exact beauty and put on a marvelous comeliness on the day when the nuptials shall be solemnized. On the day of Christ's second appearance and their resurrection, then their vile bodies shall be made like Christ's most glorious body (Philippians 3:21). Their bodies then shall have a most sparkling beauty and luster when they are transformed into the likeness of their Lord's most beautiful and glorious body. By this they will become very amiable both to Christ and to one another.

But here I am speaking of the beauty which such have who are espoused unto Christ. They are very beautiful, not externally, but internally; not in regard of their bodies, but in regard of their souls; not so much in the eyes of men as in the eyes of God. See verse 13 of this psalm: "The King's daughter is all glorious within." They have a glorious inside, which is as glorious as it is gracious; their souls are in some measure restored unto their primitive beauty; they have the most beautiful image of God engraven upon them, and as far as they are like God in knowledge, righteousness, and holiness, so far are they marvelously beautiful.

They are comparatively very beautiful. None in the world besides them have the least spark of spiritual beauty. Such as are not espoused to Christ are unrenewed, and such as are unrenewed are exceedingly spotted and defiled with sin. They have monstrous natures and hearts, most ugly, deformed spirits in the sight of God. There are indeed some spots in Christ's spouse, but there is beauty too. And they are growing farther and farther on towards perfection of beauty; and hereafter they shall be made perfect in holiness. Here they are perfect in their Head; they have a covering for their spots, I mean the perfect righteousness of Christ, through which they are reputed by God as perfectly beautiful.

5. The Lord Jesus Christ exceedingly desires the beauty of such as are espoused to Him. He greatly desires to see it, and to enjoy it in His fellowship with them. See this desire after His spouse's beauty in Song of Solomon 2:14: "O my dove, thou art in the clefts of the rock, in the secret places of the stairs, let me see thy countenance, let me hear thy voice, for sweet is thy voice, and thy countenance is comely." See further how much He admires the beauty of His spouse in 4:1: "Behold, thou art fair, my love, behold, thou art fair!" He calls His spouse His love, because she is the dear object of His love

and He admires her loveliness. He repeats it twice: "Thou art fair, thou art fair." And that with a note of admiration, "Behold, thou art fair!" and again, "Behold, thou art fair!" And then He goes on with a description of her beauty. In the 17th verse He tells her, "Thou art all fair, My love, there is no spot in thee."

Through His own comeliness which He had put upon her, He saw nothing but beauty, no spot in her. And in the 9th verse we have a wonderful expression of Christ to His spouse: "Thou hast ravished My heart, My sister, My spouse; thou hast ravished My heart with one of thine eyes, with one chain of thy neck." The original word signifies, "Thou hast un-hearted Me," or "taken away My heart from Me." The spouse had stolen away Christ's heart with one of her eyes, with her looks and glances of love upon Him. And He was exceedingly taken with the chain of faith and other graces linked together about the neck of her soul.

The Lord Jesus marvelously delights in the internal beauty of His people, and He greatly desires to see and enjoy it, which He does when they are brought near into the most intimate communion with Him.

Application

USE OF EXAMINATION
Does the Lord Jesus Christ, the King of glory, invite all the children of men, and particularly the daughters of men to be His spouse? And is He so greatly desirous of the beauty of such as are joined to Him? This, then, should put all of you upon inquiry whether you are espoused unto Jesus Christ. You have been called hereunto; have you hearkened? You have had great offers made to you; have you considered? You have been invited again and again, and many arguments have been used with you to prevail with you to come and join yourselves to the Lord Jesus; but have you inclined? Have you been persuaded? Is the match indeed made up between Christ and your souls?

If you are espoused unto Christ, then:

1. You are disjoined from sin. Is the cursed league broken which naturally exists between sin and your hearts? Before you are espoused to Christ, you are, as it were, espoused and married to sin; sin is your husband, and you are tied in its bonds. Sin inhabits you, and dwells in the embraces of your dearest love and delight. You care for the things of sin, how you may please your flesh and gratify your inordinate desires. And while this husband and beloved of your hearts lives, you are not at liberty to be espoused and married to Jesus Christ. Sin lives in the affections while it possesses the most prevailing, liking affections; and as long as you are knit and linked to sin, examine whether or not sin has yet re-

ceived its death wounds in your hearts; whether the false mask of sin has ever been plucked off, and the odiousness of it has ever been made manifest to you; whether your hearts have been brought to a loathing and detesting of it; whether sin has been killed in your affections, and the knot loosened which has tied your hearts to it. Do you indeed hate sin with the greatest and most implacable hatred? Is sin mortified and subdued as to its reigning power? If sin is dead, you are at liberty to be espoused, and it is a good sign that you are espoused to Jesus Christ.

2. If you are espoused unto Christ, then you have been drawn to Him by the Spirit. John 6:44: "No man can come unto Me, except the Father which hath sent Me draw him." You have had external calls of the Word to come unto Christ; have you been called effectually, and drawn powerfully, irresistibly, and yet most sweetly by the Spirit unto Jesus Christ? Have you had a discovery by the Spirit not only of your necessity of and lost estate without an interest in Christ, but also of His beauty and transcendent loveliness, His excellency and great willingness to entertain you in this relationship? And have you been moved and drawn hereby unto Him?

3. If you are espoused unto Christ, then you have laid hold on Him by faith. The Spirit draws unto Christ by working the grace of faith and enabling persons to believe in Him. By faith Christ is received. John 1:12: "To as many as received Him, to them gave He power to become the sons of God; even to them that believe on His name." By believing on Christ's name, people receive Christ in this relationship. Faith is the hand of the soul which

lays hold of Christ, and by this joining of the hand
with Christ the knot is tied and the soul is united to
Christ in the relationship of a spouse. Have you this
grace of faith wrought in you with power? Have you
received and applied Christ to yourselves? Have you
received Him upon His own terms? And do you by
faith draw quickening and strengthening influences from Him?

4. If you are espoused unto Christ, then you embrace Him in the arms of your dearest love; then you
love the Lord Jesus in sincerity, and you love Him
with the supremacy of your love. If you love father or
mother, houses or lands, riches or honors, delights
or pleasures, or anything in the world more than
Christ, you have no true love to Christ; be sure that
you are not espoused to Him if that is the case. But if
Christ is chiefly loved, it is an evidence that you are
joined in this relationship to Him.

5. If you are espoused unto Christ, you have acquaintance and converse with Christ, and you like
His company best; you highly value and diligently
attend upon all those ordinances which are the
means of bringing you and Christ together; this is
the great thing you desire and seek after in hearing
and prayer and the table of the Lord: that you may
have a sight of your Beloved, and a taste of His love
and more intimate communion with Him. And is
acquaintance begun with Christ, and further inti-
macy desired by you? Are pure and powerful ordinances of great esteem with you? Do you give all
diligence to wait upon and look for your Beloved in
them?

6. If you are espoused to Christ, then you en-

deavor to promote His interest and advance His name in the world. While others seek their own things, you seek the things of Jesus Christ and look upon them as your own; when others labor chiefly to lift themselves up in the esteem of men, you labor above all to lift up Christ in men's esteem. You are commending your Beloved above all others, and endeavor to bring others to love Him, and into the same relationship with Him.

Can you show such evidences as these of your espousals unto Christ. And if beyond these you have love tokens to show which you have received from Christ; if He has given you soul-refreshing visits, heart-ravishing smiles, gracious returns to your prayers, the white stone, a sight of your name written in His book, the hidden manna, the fruit of the tree of life, a glimpse of glory, an earnest of your inheritance, a foretaste of heaven, unutterable peace of conscience, a heart enlarged with love to Him and filled sometimes with the joys of the Holy Ghost—such love tokens as these may put it quite out of the question whether you are espoused unto Christ, when all these are the tokens of His conjugal, special, and most endeared love.

USE OF REPROOF

This may serve to reprove all those who refuse or neglect Christ's invitation to them to be His spouse:

1. This is your great sin, and hereby you highly affront and exceedingly offend Christ. I suppose it would offend and highly displease you if you offer your love to an inferior and have your person condemned and your love slighted by them. Christ has

offered His love and made suit unto you, who are infinitely inferior to Him. He has called upon you, and His great desire for you is that you would be His spouse. By your refusal of Him and your neglect of His person, you condemn His person and slight His love; yea, you prefer inferiors before Him, even those who are not worthy to be named with Him. And can there be a greater indignity offered? If Christ should condemn who are so mean, and slight your love as unworthy of any regard, it would not be so much wonder. It is no great wonder to see a princle slight the aspiring conjugal love of a beggar; but for you who are beggarly sinners to slight the person and love of such a Prince is a great sin and provocation.

2. This is your great folly as well as sin, to refuse and neglect the gracious offers of being made the spouse of Christ. Hereby you forfeit all that special love of His which you might have had, with all the endeared expressions thereof. By this refusal and neglect you choose rags before robes, dross before gold, pebbles before jewels, guilt before a pardon, wounds before healing, defilement before cleansing, deformity before comeliness, trouble before peace, slavery before liberty, and the service of the devil before the service of Christ. Hereby you choose honor before a crown, death before life, hell before heaven, eternal pain and misery before everlasting joy and glory. And do you need further evidence of your folly and madness in refusing and neglecting Christ's invitation to be His spouse?

USE OF COMFORT
For all those who have hearkened, considered,

and are inclined and persuaded to be the spouse of
Jesus Christ:

1. This is your wisdom: they are foolish virgins
who refuse, but you are the wise virgins who have accepted Christ's offer and have disposed yourselves
unto Him. You have made the wisest choice, and
however the blind world may deem you fools, yet you
are wise in the esteem of God, and one day will be so
in the esteem of those who now despise you.

2. This is your glory: you who are espoused unto
Jesus Christ are advanced unto great dignity and
honor. You are, of all others in the world, most
highly preferred. It is the dignity of Christ to be so
near the Father, and it is your dignity to be so near
unto Christ. It is Christ's honor beyond every creature that He is joined in the hypostatic union with
the Father, and it is your honor that you are joined
in this mystical and conjugal union and relationship to the eternal Son of God. Let not the wise man
glory in His wisdom, nor the mighty man glory in
his strength, nor the wealthy man glory in his
riches; but you may glory in the Lord that you are
espoused unto Christ. Glory not in yourselves, but in
the Lord, who has most freely and graciously taken
you into this relationship.

3. This is your safety: if you are espoused unto
Christ, you are under the wing of His special protec-
tion continually. He is, by this relationship unto
you, engaged to protect and defend you from sin
and Satan and eternal ruin. He has a special regard
for you in times of danger from men. He has secret
chambers of His providence to hide you in when
there are great storms and tempests of trouble about

you; and if such times should overtake you, which are not very unlikely, either He will preserve you from common desolation or, by it, lodge you with Himself out of the reach of all future trouble.

4. This may comfort you at all times and in all conditions: you are so nearly related unto Christ that He loves you when the world hates you, that He cares for you and has promised to provide for you what is needful here, and at length will receive you to the mansions which He has prepared in His Father's house, where you shall see and share in His glory, and take up your habitation forever with Him.

USE OF EXHORTATION

This use is for those who as yet are not espoused unto Christ as well as for those who are.

1. You who are not as yet espoused unto Christ, I shall direct my speech unto you, and that to both men and women, but particularly to you who are young women whom I am especially called now to preach to. It may be that novelty and curiosity have brought many here this day who otherwise would not have been here; and possibly the Lord may make use of this opportunity not only to invite by His Word, but also to persuade some of you by His Spirit to espouse yourselves unto Him. And if any souls may now be brought to a closure with Jesus Christ, I shall attain my great end, and both you and I shall rejoice that I hearkened unto that motion and desire which was made to me of preaching a particular sermon unto young women, as I have done many particular sermons unto young men.

Come, virgins, will you give me leave to be a

suiter unto you, not in my own name, but in the name of my Lord? May I prevail with you for your affections, and persuade you to give them unto Christ? May I be instrumental to join you and Christ together this day? Do not be coy, as some of you possibly are in other loves. Modesty and the virgin blush may very well become you when motions of another kind are made to you; but here coyness is folly and backwardness to accept this motion is a shame. And you have ten thousand times more reason to blush at your refusal of Christ as your beloved than at the acceptance, when otherwise the devil and sin would ravish your virgin affections. Never did you have a better motion made to you; never was such a match offered to you as this of being matched and espoused unto Jesus Christ.

Consider who the Lord Jesus is, to whom you are invited to espouse yourselves. He is the best husband; none is comparable to Jesus Christ.

1. Do you desire one who is great? He is of the highest dignity; none ever did or could climb into so high a feat or attain to such excellent majesty as that to which Christ is exalted. He is exalted above all the kings of the earth. Revelation 19:16: "He hath on His vesture, and on His thigh a name written, KING OF KINGS AND LORD OF LORDS." Yea, He is exalted above the angels of heaven, and none have such authority (1 Peter 3:22). "Who is gone into heaven; angels, and authorities, and powers being made subject unto Him." He is the firstborn of every creature; by whom and for whom all things were created. He is before all things, and by Him all things do consist. He is the Head of the Church, the

beginning, the firstborn from the dead, and as over all persons, so in all things He hath the pre-eminence" (Colossians 1:15–18). "He is the brightness of His Father's glory, the express image of His person" (Hebrews 1:3). He is the glory of heaven, the darling of eternity, admired by angels, dreaded by devils, and adored by saints. If the meanest beggar should be matched unto the greatest earthly prince who ever lived, it would not be such an advancement unto her as for you to be espoused unto the Lord Jesus Christ, the King of glory, whose honor and dignity you will partake of in and by this relationship.

2. Do you desire one who is rich? None is comparable unto Christ, who is the heir of all things (Hebrews 1:2), in whom all the fullness dwells (Colossians 1:19). Not only the fullness of the earth belongs to Him (Psalm 24:1), but also the fullness of heaven is at His disposal, all things being given and delivered unto Him by the Father (John 3:35 and Matthew 11:26). The riches of grace and the riches of glory are at His disposal. In Him are hidden all treasures (Colossians 2:3). The Apostle speaks of the unsearchable riches of Christ (Ephesians 3:8). The riches of Christ are unsearchable in regard to their worth; they are inestimable; the value of them is past finding out.

And they are unsearchable in regard to the abundance of them. They are inexhaustible; none can draw Christ's fountain dry; none can search and find out the bottom of Christ's treasury. If you are espoused unto Christ, you shall share in His unsearchable riches; you shall receive of His fullness—

grace for grace here and glory for glory hereafter. And He will make all needful provisions for your outward man while your abode is here in this world.

3. Do you desire one who is wise? There is none comparable unto Christ for wisdom. His knowledge is infinite and His wisdom corresponds. Solomon exceeded all who went before him or who followed after him in wisdom; but he did not so far exceed a man of the meanest wit and most shallow capacity as he was exceeded by Jesus Christ. Christ is not only wise, but wisdom (Matthew 11:19). He is the wisdom of God (1 Corinthians 1:24). Christ is infinitely wise in Himself, and He is the spring of all true, spiritual, and heavenly wisdom, which is derived unto any of the children of men. Colossians 2:3: "In Him are hid all the treasures of wisdom and knowledge." If you are espoused unto Christ, He will guide and counsel you and make you wise unto salvation.

4. Do you desire one who is potent, who may defend you against your enemies, and against any kind of injuries and abuses? There is none equal to Christ in power. Others have some power, but Christ has all power (Matthew 28:18). Others may be potent, but Christ is omnipotent; others have power, but Christ is power, the power of God (1 Corinthians 1:24). And if you are espoused to Christ, His infinite power is engaged in your defense against your enemies. He will subdue your iniquities (Micah 7:19) by that power whereby He is able to subdue all things (Philippians 3:21). He will bruise Satan under your feet (Romans 16:20). He will keep you from the evil of the world (John 17:15). He will make you more than conquerors over all your spiritual enemies,

who, without His help, would not only abuse and injure you, but also ruin and destroy you (Romans 8:37).

5. Do you desire one who is good? There is none like Christ in this regard. Others may have some goodness, but it is imperfect. Christ's goodness is complete and perfect. He is full of goodness, and in Him dwells no evil. He is good and He does good; and if you are espoused unto Christ, however bad you are by nature, He will make you in some measure good like Himself.

6. Do you desire one who is beautiful? Christ is fairer than the children of men (Psalm 45:2). He is white and ruddy, the chiefest among ten thousand (Song of Solomon 5:10). His mouth is most sweet, yea, He is altogether lovely (Song of Solomon 5:16). His eyes are most sparkling. His looks and glances of love are most ravishing. His smiles are most delightful and refreshing unto the soul. Christ is the most lovely and amiable person of all others in the world. None are so accomplished in all regards as He is accomplished; and therefore He is most desirable in this relationship. However unlovely you are in yourselves, however deformed and defiled by sin, yet if you are espoused unto Christ, He will put His comeliness upon you. He will wash you in a bath made of His own blood from your defilements, and beautify you with His own image; and so you shall become exceedingly fair. And as you may have leave to delight yourselves in Christ's beauty, so He will greatly desire and delight in yours. Our text says, "Hearken, O daughter, and consider, incline thine ear . . . so shall the king greatly desire thy beauty."

7. Do you desire one who can love you? None can love you like Christ. His love is incomparable and His love is incomprehensible. His love passes all other loves, and it passes knowledge too (Ephesians 3:19). His love is first, without any beginning. His love is free, without any motive. His love is great, without any measure. His love is constant, without any change. And His love is everlasting, without any end.

It was the love of Christ which brought Him down from heaven, which veiled His divinity in a human soul and body, which put upon Him the form of a servant, which exposed Him to contempt, reproach, and many indignities. It was love which made Him subject to hunger, thirst, sorrow, and many human infirmities, which humbled Him unto death, even the painful and ignominious death of the cross. And when out of love He had finished the work of redemption on earth, as to what was needful by way of satisfaction, it was His love which carried Him back to heaven where He was before, so that He might make application of what He had purchased; that there He might make intercession for those whom He had redeemed, and prepare a place for them, even glorious mansions with Himself in the house not made with hands, which is eternal in the heavens. It is out of love that He sends such tokens to His people from heaven to earth, which He conveys through His ordinances by His Spirit unto them. And His love tokens are infinitely beyond all other love tokens in worth and excellence. Sure, then, none is so desirable as the Lord Jesus Christ for you to espouse yourselves unto. If you are espoused to Christ, He is yours—all that He is and all that He has. You shall have His heart and share in the choicest expressions of His dearest love.

And now put all these things together. The Lord Jesus Christ, being incomparable in dignity, in riches, in wisdom, in power, in goodness, in loveliness, and in love, I think you should need no other motive to persuade you to willingness to espouse yourselves to Him.

Consider that you are invited into this relationship of a spouse unto Christ. "Hearken, O daughter, and consider, incline thine ear." In these words the Lord Jesus woos you to be His spouse. We ministers have a commission from our Lord to invite you in His name to this thing. And Christ's invitations are real, general, frequent, earnest, and free.

1. Christ's invitations to you to be His spouse are real. That there is an espousal between Christ and His people is no fancy that has no ground or foundation, except in the fond mind and imagination of some fanciful men who may deem it so to be. For there is a clear foundation for it in the Scriptures. 2 Corinthians 11:2: "I have espoused you unto one husband, that I may present you as a chaste virgin unto Christ." And 1 Corinthians 6:17: "He that is joined unto the Lord is one spirit." And as the thing is real, so you are really invited to it. The Lord does not mock and dissemble with you, like some pretending lovers who dissemble love unto virgins until they have gained their affections, and then falsely and basely relinquish them, never really intending either to espouse or marry them. But the Lord really

intends the thing in His invitations to you. He is repulsed by many unto whom He makes suit for their affections, but He never cast off any whose content and affections He had gained.

2. Christ's invitations to you to be His spouse are general. All of you are invited, and none of you are excepted; none are excluded but such as exclude themselves. All sorts of persons are invited, not only such as are of the highest quality, of whom very few hearken, but also those who are of the meanest degree in the world: the poor, the blind, the lame, and the most despicable in the eyes of men are invited to the marriage supper (Luke 14:21). Upon their coming they are received into the marriage relationship unto Christ. All sorts of sinners are invited; not only those who have kept their garments from grosser spots and escaped the greater pollutions which are in the world through lust, but also the most vile and abominable sinners: such as have run with others into the same excess of riot, and wallowed like swine in the deepest mire of sin. The most notorious transgressors are invited to be Christ's spouse, and shall be as welcome as any to the embraces of His love.

3. Christ's invitations to you to be His spouse are frequent. Some will ask you once or twice, but if they are denied they will ask no more, especially if they are of superior quality, and it would be to your advantage to hearken and consent. But the Lord Jesus Christ invites not once or twice, but very frequently: He stretches forth His hand all the day long, and though you have been a gainsaying people, He still invites you. He has been a suitor unto

some of you for many years, and He is still a suitor.
And though He is so much your superior, and you
will be infinitely beholden to Him for taking you
into this relationship, not withstanding all your re-
jections and unkindnesses, He invites you again by
me this day to be His spouse.

4. Christ's invitations to you to be His spouse are
earnest. He is very importunate with you. He does
not tacitly signify His mind and willingness to accept you, which would have been an infinite condescension and sufficient encouragement for you to
apply yourselves unto Him, but He calls upon you;
and not only calls, but He calls earnestly. Yes, He
uses many arguments to persuade you, and He adds
entreaties to His invitations. He gives us ministers a
commission to beseech you to be espoused to Him.
He is very loathe to take any denial. He is very unwilling to be put off. He knocks, and knocks hard, at
the door of your hearts for entertainment. And as
earnestness and importunity in prayer prevail with
the Lord for an audience and an answer, so the
Lord's earnestness and importunity should prevail
with you to accept Him in this desirable relationship.

5. Christ's invitations to you to be His spouse are
free. He does not expect you to bring a portion and
dowry with you, as many do, yea, as most great persons do in their applications to any upon this account. They expect something answerable to their
degree and estate; but none have anything answerable to Christ's degree, and neither does He expect
anything. He has enough for you and Him too, and
you must have nothing if you would be espoused

unto Him. You must be poor, naked, and empty, and He will enrich, clothe, fill, and supply you out of His treasury with all things needful to qualify you and make you fit for Himself.

Consider that if you are once espoused to Christ, you shall never be divorced. If you are once joined into this relationship with Him, you shall never be separated from Him. Neither men nor devils shall be able to disjoin you, and when death breaks all other conjugal bonds it shall not break the conjugal bonds between you and Christ, but bring you into the most full and everlasting possession of your Beloved.

And what do you say now, young women? Shall I have a grant for my Master, or be sent away with a repulse and refusal? I think by this time you should begin to have a mind unto Jesus Christ. You look as if you desire Him; you hearken as if you would consent. What do you say? Shall the match be made up this day between Christ and your souls? May I be instrumental to join your hands, or, rather, your hearts together? May I be instrumental to tie that knot which can never be untied? Some marry in haste and repent at their leisure; but if you were once espoused to Jesus Christ, you would never repent; nothing would grieve you but that you were joined to Him no sooner, and you would not be disjoined again for all the world.

Shall this be the day of your espousals? Some of you have waited a long time, and will you defer any longer? If you will not say yes now, Christ may not say yes the next time; if you refuse now when Christ calls and invites, Christ may refuse when you call

and entreat. This may be the last time He asks, and
therefore it is dangerous to refuse. Some of you are
very young, too young for other espousals, but none
of you are too young for this espousal unto Jesus
Christ. In other espousals you must have the consent
of parents, but in this you are at your own disposal.
You may, and must, match yourselves to Christ
whether parents consent or not.

QUESTION. But what shall we do that we may be
espoused unto Jesus Christ?

ANSWER 1. Be sensible of your need of Christ
and this espousal unto Him, without which you are
slaves to sin and Satan, children of wrath, hated by
God here and in danger of eternal ruin in the other
world. And therefore there is a necessity of this relationship to Christ that you may hereby be interested
in His redemption and salvation.

ANSWER 2. Labor for longing desires after this
relationship with Christ. He desires that you would
be His spouse; and do you desire that you may be espoused to Him? Desire it chiefly and earnestly, and
for this end consider the motives which I have
spread before you to excite your desires after Christ.

ANSWER 3. Diligently seek this relationship to
Christ; attend upon the ordinances which God has
appointed to be the means of bringing and joining
you and Christ together, such as hearing the Word,
prayer, and so on. Seek Christ in hearing, and rest
not in the outside of the duty; cry mightily to God in
prayer that He would draw you and join you by His
Spirit unto His Son.

ANSWER 4. Put off your filthy garments. I am not
speaking of the garments on your bodies, but of the

filthy rags of sin which are on your souls. You must lay aside all filthiness and superfluity of naughtiness, all pride, envy, malice, worldliness, inordinate affection, evil concupiscence, and every other defiling lust. These are the old clothes of the old man which must be put off if you would be espoused unto Christ.

ANSWER 5. Put on the white raiment and clean garments and rich robes which Christ has provided for you. I mean the attire of grace, the robes of His perfect righteousness; in these garments you will be beautiful and accepted.

ANSWER 6. Reach forth the hand of faith and lay hold of Him. Consent that you will have Him; receive Him on His own terms, and He is yours forever.

ANSWER 7. Devote yourselves to Him body, soul, and all. Be His forever, and then you may say, "My Beloved is mine, and I am His." And then you will be happy that you were ever born!

Now to you who are already espoused to Jesus Christ:

1. Admire and adore that rich and free grace which has chosen and brought you into this relationship. Say, "Not unto us, not unto us, but unto Thy name be the praise!" Say, "Oh, wonderful! wonderful! wonderful love! that we should be made the spouse of Christ! We who had no beauty! We who had no dowry! that we who embraced dunghills should be taken into the embraces of the Lord! Oh, infinite, condescending kindness!"

2. See that you give reverence unto Christ to

whom you are espoused. He is your Lord, and you must reverence and stand in awe of Him. Take heed of pride, passion, discontent with your condition, murmurings under affliction, and every other sin which is displeasing to Christ, and which is unbecoming the reverence you owe to Him.

3. Be loving and faithful unto Christ. Receive not any creature in the world into the embraces of that dearest love which belongs to your espoused husband. Love Him supremely, love Him ardently, and labor to increase in love to Him daily.

4. Be subject unto Christ, careful to please Him in everything. Be ready to yield universal obedience to whatsoever He shall reveal to you to be His will.

5. Endeavor to maintain daily communion with Him in His ordinances. Do not desire the ordinances for themselves, but for the sake of Christ. Grieve when He withdraws and is absent; rejoice when He draws near and manifests His patience.

6. Look for, long for, and prepare for Christ's second appearance, when the nuptials between you shall be solemnized, and you are taken to live forever with Him in mansions of everlasting joys.

The Best Gift

God's call upon young men for their hearts

"My son, give me thine heart." Proverbs 23:26

Solomon was not only a king, but a prophet; not only a prince, but a preacher. And in the name of God He calls upon all the children of men, especially young men, by the name of His Son, for their heart, that they would present the Lord with the gift of the heart. As in the later clause of the verse he directs the eye of their mind unto the observation of God's way, which he calls his way ("let thine eye observe my ways"), so in this first clause he directs their hearts unto God Himself, whom he represents ("My son, give me thine heart"). Hence observe:

DOCTRINE: All men, especially young men, ought to give their hearts unto God.

In handling this point I shall show what is meant by the heart; what it is to give God the heart; why all men, especially young men, ought to give God their hearts; and make some application.

1. What is meant by the heart? The heart in Scripture is frequently taken for the whole soul, including all its powers and faculties. Thus Matthew 15:8: "This people draweth nigh unto Me with their mouth, and honoreth Me with their lips." The wor-

ship of the outward man was there, "but their hearts
are far from Me." The worship of the soul and inward man was lacking. So Romans 2:28–29: "He is
not a Jew which is one outwardly, neither is that circumcision which is outward in the flesh; but he is a
Jew which is one inwardly, and circumcision is that
of the heart in the Spirit." And we shall find in
Scripture that every faculty is sometimes called by
the title of "the heart." The understanding—
Ephesians 4:18: "Being alienated from the life of
God, through the ignorance that is in them because
of the blindness of their hearts." The conscience—1
John 3:20: "For if our heart condemns us, God is
greater than our hearts, and knoweth all things."
The memory—Luke 2:19: "Mary kept all these things
in her heart." But chiefly, and most properly, the
heart is taken in Scripture for the will and affections
which are seated in the heart; things such as the
understanding, the memory, the fancy, and the
imagination are all seated under this heading. And
thus we may understand the acceptance of the word
"heart" in this place as meaning namely the will and
affections, yet not excluding the other faculties.

    2. What is it to give God the heart? Persons give
God their hearts when their wills choose Him as
their chief Good, when they place their liking affections chiefly upon Him; when their love is chiefly
towards Him, their desires chiefly after Him, their
hopes and delights chiefly in Him. Persons give God
their hearts when they open the door of these secret
chambers and let God in and give Him the dearest
embraces of their affections; when they give Him
full possession of their hearts, and set Him up in the

highest room; when they give God the chief rule and command in their hearts, placing Him upon the throne; when they engage their hearts to the Lord in a solemn covenant to be His and His alone.

3. Why should all men, especially young men, give their hearts unto God?

REASON 1. Because God has a right to their hearts. The devil and sin have the possession, but they have no right to the heart. They are usurpers, and therefore should be turned out. God alone has the right to the heart, and that to the heart of young ones as well as others. Young ones do not have the right to possess their inheritance left to them by their fathers while they are under the age of twenty-one; but God has the right to possess the hearts of young ones while they are minors. He has a right to their hearts as soon as they are born, as soon as they have a heart, and that because He has made them and bought them. They belong to Him by right of creation and by right of purchase.

The body was formed by God, but the soul is infused and comes more immediately out of His hands; and it is only fair to return to God that which He has made, to present God with the gift of that which is His own, the work of His own hands, especially when besides His natural right to the heart He has made a purchase of it; He has laid down a great price for it, even the price of His Son's blood. As the blood of Christ has purchased an everlasting inheritance for men, so it has purchased the hearts of men for God to be His everlasting habitation. See this argument urged by the Apostle upon the Corinthians in 1 Corinthians 6:19–20: "Ye are not your own, for ye are bought with a price; therefore, glorify God in your body and in your spirit which are God's." God has a double right both to the body and the spirit too. And as the heart is His by way of right, so all ought to make it His by way of tender and gift.

REASON 2. All, especially young men, ought to give God their hearts because God requires them. Some tacitly give away their right by not demanding it; and some things which are the right of such a man yet are not his without a lawful demand. But God has not only right to the heart, but He requires it; He makes a demand of it; He commands us to give it. See Matthew 22:37–38: "Thou shalt love the Lord thy God with all thy heart, and all thy soul, and all thy mind: this is the first and great commandment." It is not the eye, ear, tongue, or knee that God cares for, but the heart. The sincere and supreme love of the heart is the chief and most comprehensive commandment. Some debts are forfeited by law if, though they are demanded, they are not timely demanded; but God timely demands this debt of the heart. He does not wait till men have grown into older years, but He demands their hearts when they are young. He calls upon young men to give their hearts, as the text says, "My son, give Me thine heart."

REASON 3. All, especially young men, ought to give God their hearts because God will accept their hearts. If a man will not accept his right, he loses his right; and there is no obligation upon a man to accept a gift that is despised. But God will accept the heart, and nothing is more acceptable than the heart; nothing is acceptable like the heart; and nothing is acceptable without the heart. All the good language of the lips, the devotion of the knees and all other bodily exercise, is of no worth in God's account. All is flattery; all is mockery without the heart. The sacrifices under the law, though of God's own appointment, compared to the sacrifice of the heart will not be esteemed; and without the sacrifice of the heart they were despised. But the heart was never despised, never refused, but readily accepted as the most delightful sacrifice. See Psalm 51:16–17: "For Thou desirest not sacrifice (that is, comparatively), else would I give it; Thou delightest not in burnt offerings, the sacrifices of God are a broken spirit; a broken and contrite heart, O God, Thou wilt not despise."

God does not despise the heart, yea, He desires and delights in the sacrifice of the heart when it is offered up to Him by the hands of Christ, our great High Priest in heaven. A heart broken and bleeding for sin, gasping and breathing after God, is very pleasing and acceptable. And as God will accept the hearts of any, so especially the hearts of young ones. The sooner any bring their hearts unto God, the better He is pleased. The rose is sweetest in the bud before it is quite blown; and the love of youths to God has a great fragrance, and is very sweet and delightful to Him.

REASON 4. All, especially young men, ought to give God their hearts because He deserves them; not only as He has a right to them, but also as He is the most deserving object. Nothing is worthy of your hearts besides Him, or in the least degree worthy in comparison to Him.

If loveliness deserves love, God is altogether lovely. This cannot be said of any creature in the world which may be apt to draw away the heart. The creatures indeed may have loveliness, but the loveliness of creatures is inferior. God's loveliness is supreme. The loveliness of creatures is defective; God's loveliness is perfect. The creatures may have some loveliness, but God has all loveliness. The creature's loveliness is derivative; God's loveliness is from Himself, and whatever loveliness the creatures have they derive it from Him. Therefore, even *that* loveliness is eminently in Him, and moreover such loveliness as is infinitely beyond that. What is the beam in comparison to the sun? What is the stream in comparison to the fountain? What is the drop in comparison to the ocean? And what is a creature's loveliness in comparison to the Creator's loveliness?

Indeed, God's loveliness is not visible, like some creature's loveliness, because God is a Spirit and His loveliness is spiritual. But God's loveliness is not the less because it is not corporal and visible, but all the more because it is not so low and inferior, and subject to alterations as bodily beauty is. As the beauty of the mind adorned with wisdom and grace is far beyond the beauty of the body of the rarest symmetry and mixture of colors, so the beauty of God, which is spiritual, infinitely excels all created beauty, whether of body or of mind.

God's loveliness cannot be discerned with the eye of the body, but it may be viewed with the eye of the mind, with the eye of faith, through the illuminations of the Spirit. Indeed, the beauty of His face cannot be seen by any in the body; this vision is only fit for angels, and is reserved for the saints in heaven. Yet in His back parts there is infinitely more loveliness to be seen than in the face of any creatures whatsoever. If there could be a composite of all creature loveliness in one person, it would fall infinitely short of the loveliness of God in any one of His excellencies and perfections. Hence was that desire of David in Psalm 27:4: "One thing have I desired of the Lord, that will I seek after, that I may dwell in the house of the Lord all the days of my life, to behold the beauty of the Lord, and to enquire in His temple." And also Psalm 63:1–2: "O God, Thou art my God; early will I seek Thee, my soul thirsteth for Thee, my flesh longeth for Thee, as in a dry and thirsty land where no water is; to see Thy power and Thy glory, so as I have seen Thee in the sanctuary."

If suitableness deserves love, there is infinitely more of this in God to the heart than in anything else that anyone might set their hearts upon. Indeed, sensitive objects are more suitable to the brutish part, I mean the senses, in which many brutes excel men. But God is most suitable to the most excellent and noble part of man, which is the soul. He is a suitable good, and the only suitable good for the heart because He is the only chief Good. Nothing beneath, nothing besides the chief Good, can give true satisfaction to the soul. None but God can fill up the large and immense desires of the heart. The house may be filled with goods, the bags may be filled with silver and gold, the cabinets may be filled with jewels, but none of these things can fill the heart. The eye may be tired of seeing, the ear weary of hearing, and all the senses glutted and cloyed with their proper ob-

jects; but none of these objects are suitable to the
soul, and therefore cannot fill and satisfy its desires.

Earthly riches are uncertain and thorny; worldly
honors are vain and windy; sensual pleasures are
thin and empty; and all are of short continuance
and very transitory. What, then, can they all do to
give satisfaction to a rational soul, which is a spiritual substance? What can they give to an immortal
soul—which must abide when the body is dropped
off into the dust, and all these things are vanished
out of sight—and which must live as long as the
eternal God shall live?

God is the only suitable good for the soul; the
creatures are not so far beneath the soul as God is
above it; the creatures do not have as much emptiness as God has fulness; the creatures do not have
such insufficiency as God has all-sufficiency. He
who is self-sufficient must be all-sufficient. An ocean
surely is sufficient to fill a bucket or a nutshell.
Though ten thousand worlds are not sufficient to
fill one soul, yet one God who is all-sufficient can
fill ten thousand worlds of souls. It is a great expression in Ephesians 3:20–21: "Now to Him who is able
to do exceeding abundantly above all that we ask or
think, according to the power that worketh in us; to
Him be glory." He can do above, abundantly above,
exceedingly above. In the original the words trans-
late "above abundantly."

He can do infinitely beyond not only our prayers,
what we can ask, but also our conceptions, what we
can think. We may ask for great things—mountains
of gold seats among the stars, the most delicious
things for the senses—but God can do more than

this for us; and if He does not give such things because they are not so good, He gives that which is
better. A little true grace is beyond all, and God can
do beyond what we can ask in spiritual riches. The
riches of glory are exceedingly, abundantly beyond
the riches of grace. We may conceive and think
more than we can have confidence in or find words
to ask for; but God can do for us beyond either our
desires or thoughts. Yea, there is more in Him than
we can imagine. God is a fountain of goodness
which is always running, overflowing, and ever-flow-
ing. He is a treasury of all good things which can
never be exhausted and emptied. Surely, then, God is
the most suitable good for the heart, and most deserves the heart.

*If love deserves the heart and calls for a return of love,
surely God has infinitely more of this than anyone else.* None
can match Him in loveliness, and none can match
Him in love. John 3:16: "God so loved the world that
He gave His only begotten Son." God so loved the
world; how did He love the world? There is no comparison by which to set it forth, nothing great
enough to express it; it is too big to be put into the
scales with any creature's love unless you weigh vast
mountains in one balance and a light feather in the
other. Yea, I may safely say that the smallest dust on
the ground, or the least mote that flies in the air,
may better be compared with the whole globe of the
earth for weight than the love of any creature can be
compared with the love of God to mankind. And if
you ask, therefore, how God loved mankind, the answer must not be by a comparison, for it passes both
comparison and comprehension. It is set forth by

the expression of it in giving His only begotten Son
for men, that, believing in Him, they might not perish, but have everlasting life.

Here is love, not so much in a word as in a deed;
love in a love token, love in a gift, and such a gift as
is invaluable; a gift so necessary that without it eternal ruin could not be avoided; so beneficial that by
it and with it eternal life and happiness is obtained.
God's love is so great in giving His Son that when
the Apostle John speaks of it, he tells us not only
that God *has* love, but that God *is* love. 1 John 4:9–10:
"God is love; in this was manifested the love of God
towards us, because God sent His only begotten Son
into the world that we might live through Him.
Herein is love, not that we loved God, but that He
loved us, and sent His Son to be a propitiation for
our sins."

Creatures have love; it is a quality in them, and it
has degrees. The highest capacity we have for love is
but as it is a quality, and even in that which we are
capable of we are deficient while in this world. But
love in God is not a quality, for a quality is an acci-
dent, and there are no accidents in God. Therefore
it is His essence: "God is love." There is a depth in
the expression which we cannot fathom. If the
Apostle cries out in Romans 11:33: "O the depth of
the riches both of the wisdom and knowledge of
God! How unsearchable are His judgments, and His
ways past finding out!" we may also cry out in an ec-
stasy of admiration, "O the depth of the riches of the
goodness and love of God! How unsearchable are
His mercies, and the ways of His grace past finding
out!"

We may apprehend something of God's love, but we cannot comprehend it. Whoever did or could look into the depth of God's heart? The heart of man is deep, but the heart of God is far deeper; and indeed, in comparison to God, the streams of our love are but small brooks and shallow rivulets to the deep current and bottomless ocean of love in the heart of God to sinners through Jesus Christ. God's love is, first, free, tender, unchangeable, from everlasting to everlasting.

But I must not launch too deeply into this subject of God's love, which, in many discourses by those who have the most elevated apprehensions and sweetest tastes of it, cannot be set forth with any suitableness unto its greatness. Now such love of God surely deserves the heart, and the return of the choicest and chief affections which the children of men can possibly present Him. Love usually draws forth particular and endeared love more than loveliness; but when such infinite loveliness, suitableness, and, withal, such infinite, incomparable love meet in one God, surely we must say that He is the most deserving object of that love.

REASON 5. All, especially young men, ought to give their hearts to God because He will best use their hearts. Their hearts will be abused by anything they give them to unless it is God alone. If they give their hearts to the world, it will debase and degrade them; but if they give their hearts unto God He will advance and ennoble them. If the creatures have their hearts, they will impoverish them; but if God has their hearts, He will enrich them. If sin gets their hearts, it will deform them; but if God gets their hearts, He will beautify them. If lust is received into their hearts, it will defile them; but if God is received into their hearts, He will cleanse them. If God does not have the heart, the devil, the world, and lust will possess it; and be sure they will abuse it. It is a thousand times better to entertain God in the heart than any other inhabitant. He has promised to dwell where He is entertained. 2 Corinthians 6:16: "For ye are the temple of the living God, as God hath said, 'I will dwell in you, and walk in you.' " And be sure He will use the heart well where He dwells.

The devil and lust make the heart a dungeon, but God's presence makes the heart a palace. God has two palaces: the one is the highest heavens, the other is the lowest hearts; and where God dwells He will bring His own furniture. He will throw out of doors the rotten furniture of sin which He finds and bring in the furniture of grace. He will, as it were, hang the heart with the rich tapestry and curious embroidery of the Spirit that He may take delight in His habitation adorned with His own ornaments.

And He will bring in His own provisions, too, and feast them with His love and the kindest expressions thereof. These shall yield such peace and satisfaction, such comfort and sweetness, and sometimes such ravishing joys, as have not entered into the hearts of the carnal and worldly to conceive. Moreover, He will watch over the heart and defend it from many mischiefs and dangers, from many snares and temptations, from many sins, and those ruins which sin leads the godly into.

To conclude, by the grace which He gives the heart here, He will qualify and prepare it for glory hereafter. And at length, when the soul now given to Him shall be separated from the body, it shall not lack a habitation, for He will receive it into the dearest closets and eternal embraces of His love. Surely, then, God will best use the heart, and therefore all should give their hearts unto Him.

Application

USE OF INFORMATION
Hence learn that none have the disposal of their own hearts; none have liberty to give their hearts as they please; to choose, love, desire, or delight in what or in whom they please. It is the speech of the ungodly, "Our lips are our own, who is Lord over us?" (Psalm 12:4). And it is a more ungodly speech to say, "Our hearts are our own, who is Lord over us?" There is nothing which any man calls their own, properly and strictly, unless it is sin. Whatever any are or have, they owe it to God from whom they have received it. But, above all, God claims His right to the heart, and He is most jealous of the heart. None may give away their hearts since they rightly belong to Him.

Learn here that God has disposed of our hearts better than we could or would dispose of them ourselves. If God had not directed our hearts to Himself and commanded us to give them to Him, we would foolishly dispose of them to inferior things, which are wholly unworthy of them, and which would woefully abuse them. All people so dispose their hearts who give no heed to this command.

Learn here that God has made that to be our duty, to give our hearts to Him, which is our great privilege, to give our hearts to Him. This commandment surely is not grievous, but most reasonable and sweet. God is not beholding to us for our hearts, but we are beholding to Him for accepting them.

Learn here the difference between the wicked and the righteous. The difference does not lie in their riches; for when many of the righteous are poor in this world, multitudes of wicked men abound in wealth. It does not lie in worldly grandeur and dignity, for usually the wicked are advanced to the highest seats of honor, and are esteemed while the righteous are low and in disgrace. It does not lie in their food and apparel. Dives is arrayed in purple and fine linen, faring deliciously every day, while Lazarus lies at his gate hungry and in rags. It does not lie in any beauty and strength of body, in any natural parts or acquired abilities of mind; some who have very foul insides are outwardly fair and beautiful. Many are ignorant of the mysteries of salvation who are great scholars in other things, and of high esteem for worldly wisdom and prudence, while the righteous, many of them, have a contemptible outside and are of very mean, natural, and acquired abilities.

Rather, the difference between the righteous and the wicked, and wherein the righteous excel the wicked in the world, is in the disposing of their hearts. The wicked give their hearts to the creature: some to the dung of earthly riches, others to the filth of sensual delight, others to the wind of worldly esteem. Some give their hearts to their friends, others to their lands, others to their hawks and hounds, and all the wicked are of such a low and inferior spirit that they let their hearts sink beneath themselves unto something that debases them. But the righteous lift up their hearts to Him who is above them, whereby they are advanced. They dispose their hearts unto God, who is the chief Good. When the streams of the wicked man's affections run downwards, theirs run upwards. And surely of all others they have the greatest wisdom and true heighth and nobleness of spirit whose hearts are raised so high as to be joined unto the Lord.

USE OF REPROOF

This reproves those who give away their hearts, but not to God. Are there not too many of these? God has your ears sometimes, and your lips and knees sometimes, and your bodies, it may be, are often presented before Him in religious duties; but has God your hearts? Have you presented God with this gift, with this sacrifice, without which all other sacrifices of your lips and outward devotion are but a vain oblation? They are then despised and an abomination to Him.

Young men, you are disposed of by your friends, some to this calling and some to that; but friends do not have the disposal of your hearts. You have disposal of them yourselves, and have not too many of you disposed away your hearts from God to the creature? Have not vanity and the world, and some foolish, filthy, and deceitful lust the chief room and possession of your hearts? God has called for your hearts, but you have not hearkened. God has knocked at the door, but you have not opened. He has in His Word and by His Spirit wooed for your chief affections, but you have hitherto given Him a denial and rejection. When you have listened to the devil, and readily opened your hearts to the world, and given your dearest loves and delights to the creatures, you have been deaf to God, and your hearts have been shut up against Him. You have foolishly withheld your affections from Him. Oh, consider the great sin herein!

1. You who give your hearts to something other than God are guilty of heart-idolatry. That which you chiefly love, desire, and delight yourselves in is your god. If it is meat and drink for your belly, your belly is your god. Philippians 3:19: "Whose god is their belly." If it is gold and silver, the riches of the world, riches are your god. And therefore covetousness is called idolatry. Colossians 3:5: "Covetousness, which is idolatry." Whatever it is that you supremely love is your god and the idol of your hearts, if it is anything beneath and besides the true God. And can any of these gods hear your prayers? Can they save you in your troubles if you call upon them? Can they deliver you from the wrath to come? Can they abide with you to be your eternal portion?

2. You who give your hearts to something other than God are guilty of spiritual adultery. Your Maker is, or should be, your Husband; and you go a-whoring from Him when you give your hearts chiefly to any person or thing besides Him. You commit spiritual adultery with any creature which you receive into the embraces of your dearest affec-

tions. And therefore those whose hearts are chiefly
addicted to the world and to its friendship are called
adulterers and adulteresses. James 4:4: "Ye adulterers
and adulteresses, know ye not that the friendship of
the world is enmity with God?"

3. You who give your hearts to anything other
than God are guilty of great injustice. Your hearts
rightly belong to God, as has been proven. He has
made them and He has bought them; and you may
as justly give away money which belongs to another,
or goods or houses or lands which belong to
another, as to give away your hearts to any other
which rightly belong unto God.

4. You who give your hearts to anything other
than God are guilty of great folly. You are hereby not
only unjust towards God, but you are injurious towards yourselves. God has no need of your hearts,
but you need to give them to Him. Your loss is great;
by withholding your hearts from God you lose the
heart of God which you would have in exchange; you
lose the favor of God, which is infinitely beyond the
favor of men; you lose the peace of conscience
which is the soul's feast; you lose the joys of the Holy
Ghost, which are unspeakably sweet and glorious;
you lose all that communion with God, and com-
munications of the richest spiritual treasures which
you might have from God if you give your hearts
unto Him. And hereby you lose your souls, which is
the greatest loss; you lose your salvation, and the
eternal crown and glory which you are capable of.

And what do you gain by giving your hearts to
something other than God? You look indeed for
great satisfaction and delight, and a happiness

which the things you chiefly desire and love might yield to you; but be sure you will be disappointed, for none of these things can give that which they do not have. Oh, there is something indeed which you will gain by giving your hearts to the creatures: namely deep wounds of conscience, heart-piercing sorrows, smarting scourges of afflictions. Or, if your life is more pleasant and conscience sleeps for awhile, at the end of your life you are likely to be consumed with terrors. Or, if you are not awakened then, be sure you will be awakened in the flames of hell, fire and brimstone, and a horrible tempest of God's wrath. His most dreadful indignation will be the eternal portion which you will gain by preferring the creature above God in your affections. And what can be more foolish, more injurious to you than this sin?

USE OF EXHORTATION

Let this exhort all men, especially you who are young men, to give your hearts unto God. This is the first day of the new year, and some of you bring New Year's gifts to one another; be persuaded to present God with the New Year's gift of your hearts. The devil, that old serpent, and the world, that old cheat, has had your hearts all the old year; and some deceitful lusts have hitherto gained and possessed your affections. Be persuaded to call off and pluck your hearts now at length out of the hands of these enemies who seek your destruction. Be persuaded to offer your hearts to God for a New Year's gift this New Year's day, and as a new and living sacrifice which will be very acceptable to the God of your salvation.

Some of you have nothing of your own which you
can give unto men without wronging your masters
or your parents; but all of you have hearts of your
own which you may give to God, and which you
cannot keep from Him without wronging Him and
yourselves too.

Young men, perhaps you have given your hearts
to delight and pleasure, the goddess which most in
the world adore; but sit down and consider whether
sensual pleasure deserves your hearts. You have
tasted a little of its sweetness, and hope for a great
deal more, yea, as much as shall give satisfaction
and contentment; but you will find emptiness and
vanity in the enjoyment, bitterness and misery to be
the consequences of that pleasure your hearts love
and desire so much.

Solomon, who had as great a confluence of creature delights as any man living, upon trial, found all
to be vanity and vexation of spirit. From his own experience, he warns young men against indulging
the flesh and giving their hearts to any sensual delights. Indeed, he seems in his first words to allow
young men to take their pleasures, and to walk in
the way of their hearts. But his speech is ironic, for
withal he tacitly intimates how dearly they will pay
for their pleasures when God brings them to judgment. Ecclesiastes 11:9: "Rejoice, O young man, in
thy youth, and let thine heart cheer thee in the days
of thy youth, and walk in the ways of thy heart, and
in the sight of thine eyes; but know that for all these
things God will bring thee unto judgment."

It is as if Solomon had said, "Young ones, be as
merry and frolicking as you will; take your fill of

sensual pleasures if you think they are good; smell every flower, taste and feed on every dainty dish; drink, and drink deep of every sweet cup. Bathe yourselves in the streams of all creature delights; run into every pleasant embrace; melt away in soft pleasures; indulge your sensual appetite to the height; gratify every lust to the full; withhold yourselves from nothing which is pleasing to the flesh; do whatever seems good in your own eyes; be cheerful and rejoice all your youthful days; seek, gather, and enjoy with all freedom whatever is delightful to your hearts or pleasant to your eyes. Do this, if you think it is good, and if it is in your interest. BUT KNOW THIS: for all these things, God will bring you into judgment!"

Believe, remember, and seriously consider that there is a day of reckoning not far off, a day of judgment coming, when you will be called to an account; and when all your delights and pleasures will vanish like the cloud and will have fled forever out of your sight, then your sweetest delights will be turned into gall and wormwood. Then horrible pain and everlasting torment will take the place of your momentary pleasures—and as you like the one, so indulge yourselves in the other.

Or, it may be, it is the honor and esteem of men which too many of you who are young are most enamored with, and have addicted your hearts to. Some of you, though you have not the golden chain around your neck, have gotten the chain of pride and ambition around your heart, whereby it is captivated and led away from God unto any kind of practices which are likely to get you a name and raise your esteem from others. And is it not to be feared that some of you make use of religion as a footstool to raise you a little higher, or as a stirrup to advance you into the seat of some kind of repute, or as a cloak to cover ambitious designs? And is any kind of honor, either among the ungodly or the religious, worthy of your hearts? Does it deserve the highest place in your affections? Is it fit that pride should sit in the throne which belongs to God? Your affections are hungry; will they be satisfied with wind? If they are filled sometime, will they, can they herewith be satisfied? Do you not lose honor by loving it and desiring it inordinately? and that higher honor than the honor which you may desire, but never attain to?

I mean, do you not lose the honor and esteem of God, which is infinitely beyond all the highest honor and esteem of men? Honor is not in him who is honored, but in him who honors; and is that so amiable which is not in yourselves, but in another's breast? Or, if you desire honor, is worldly honor the most desirable, which is of all things the most uncertain and inconsistent? Is any honor so sure and so great as the honor which the great Jehovah has for all who truly love and fear Him? And what sweetness can you really find in others' good esteem of you when you have so much reason to disesteem yourselves? Must not the esteem of you be for low and inferior things which are not praiseworthy, or else must not their esteem be built upon a mistake? And can you take any great comfort in a mistake? Can this be a happiness and chief good for a rational soul?

Suppose that your ambition was gratified, and
you advanced not only in esteem, but also in a high
place of dignity; are not all high places very slip-
pery? And by however much your place is the higher,
would not your fall be the lower? If you were kings or
emperors, death would quickly turn off your crowns,
and pluck your robes off your backs and your
scepters out of your right hands. And what honor do
the worms give to the bodies of great ones when
they are brought down to the dust? What honor will
God give to the souls of wicked great ones when they
are out of the body? What honor will the Lord Jesus
give to such at the last day, when He appears with
His glorious train of angels to judge the world in
righteousness? Will not all the honor of wicked
men be then turned into shame, disgrace, everlasting contempt, and confusion of face? And is it good,
then, to set your heart upon honor instead of God?

Or, it may be, young ones, that your hearts are
not upon the wing to carry you either to the mountains of pleasures or the mountains of honor; but
they are groveling upon the earth. You are under it
and are digging for mines and treasures there. I
mean, perhaps your hearts are more addicted to
gaining earthly riches; and are they more worthy of
your hearts than is God? Can they yield more satisfaction unto you, or abide more surely by you, than
those pleasures or honors of the world which I have
been endeavoring to disgrace? If you had gold like
the dust, silver like the sand, and jewels like the
stones of the field; if you had as much wealth as your
hearts could wish, could you find the contentment
your hearts desire in any of these things? Besides, if

riches in great abundancc could give contentment (which they cannot), are you certain to get such an abundance? Has the world treasures enough to enrich all who so dearly love and desire it? Are not the times hard? Is not trading low? Is it not with great difficulty that any get an estate? Do not such as will be rich run themselves into temptations and snares which entangle them, and enslave themselves to many hurtful and foolish lusts, which at length undo and drown them in perdition and destruction (1 Timothy 6:9)? Read and consider what the wise man says in Proverbs 23:5: "Wilt thou set thine eyes upon that which is not? For riches certainly make themselves wings; they flee away like an eagle towards heaven."

Will you set your hearts upon that which is not what it seems to be, or which is of such a short life it virtually has no being? Riches certainly make themselves wings; like eagles they fly away from you. And will you make yourselves wings, and like eagles fly after them? Are you likely to overtake them when they are upon the wing to be gone? And when they are gone upon the wing, will they return again? Or if they should abide as long as you abide, will not death make wings for you ere long, upon which, willing or unwilling, you must fly away and leave all your riches behind?

Think how death will strip you of all your wealth, and bereave you of all your riches. Naked you came into the world, and naked you must return. And think how grievous it will be for you to part with those things unto which you have given your hearts. Will it not be a tearing to your hearts to be so disjoined from that unto which they are now so glued, especially when you think that you must not only leave all that you love so much, but also must go to a place of most exquisite and eternal torments in hell which you fear so much?

Let me then persuade all of you, especially you who are young men, to call your hearts off from all these things which the devil uses as bait to catch hearts, as snares to entangle and captivate affections. Look through the bait to the hook; look to the prison where the devil, in such chains which he has laid upon your affections, is leading you; withdraw your hearts from the world and everything therein, and present them now to the Lord. The Lord has sent me this day to woo your hearts. Oh, that I could win your hearts for Him!

You are young men, and most of you, if not all, are single men. Suppose that the most lovely young woman that ever your eyes beheld, of such stature, feature, and exact mixture of colors as you never saw anyone so beautiful before; suppose her birth and dowry to be so far above you; suppose her to be humble like the ground, and of the sweetest disposition so that none are like her; and this person should make an offer of particular and most ardent love unto any of you, and be willing to give herself and all that she has to you. The only thing she expected in return was love on your part. I suppose there is not a one of you who would refuse and withhold your love.

But what is any creature in comparison to God? Not so much as the dust on a scale! His excellencies are infinitely beyond compare and comprehension.

I have set forth the loveliness of the Lord as being infinitely beyond all creature loveliness.

I have set forth His suitableness unto your souls, and withal His infinite love; and by me He makes an offer of Himself and His love to you, to the meanest and most unworthy among you. But He looks for a return of love on your part. By me He calls for your heart. Think what an indignity it will be to the Lord, what a folly and injury to yourselves, should you refuse and withhold your hearts from Him. By me, God calls for your hearts; they are His due. If anyone else can claim such right to them, let them have them; if anyone else desires or deserves them so much, let them have them; if anyone else can so advance, beautify, enrich, satisfy, and fill them with such peace and joy; let them have them.

No, no, there is no person who can do it! Nothing in this world can do it, and will you still withhold your hearts from God? Why are you so backward to bestow your affections upon God? Why are you so loathe to give your hearts to Him who has given you your hearts, who has given you all that you are and all that you have, who has given His Son for you, who offers to give His Son to you, and with Him pardon, peace, many special favors here, and the kingdom of heaven hereafter?

What do you say, young men? Shall God have your hearts or not? God not only calls for them and will accept them, but He is loathe to be denied. By me, He entreats and beseeches you so that He might have them. In His entreaties to you, so that you would be reconciled to Him, He entreats you to give Him your hearts. God is reconciled to you when He

gives His Son to you, and you are reconciled to Him
when you give Him your hearts. Then your enmity
against Him is laid aside.

See how God entreats by ministers for this in
2 Corinthians 5:20: "Now we are ambassadors for
Christ, as if God did beseech you by us, we pray you,
in Christ's stead, be ye reconciled unto God." Hear,
O heavens! Wonder, O angels! Admire, O saints! Be
astonished, O sinners! Be confounded, O devils!
God is not only willing to accept hearts, but desires
them! He not only calls for them, but entreats them!
That God should entreat His creatures! Entreat sinners, traitors, rebels, persons so mean and vile! And
when He has no need of them, that He should entreat them, as if He were beholden to them to give
entreaties! O wonderful, wonderful condescension!
Although you have stopped your ears so long, and
refused Him your hearts so often, yet the Lord still
entreats. And He would fain prevail with you for this
gift so beneficial, not to Him to receive it, but to you
to give it. Upon my knees, if that would do it, I would
beseech you in the name of my Lord that you would
give your hearts unto God.

I think you should not shut your ears to such
kind invitations, or, when your ears are open, I
think you should not shut your hearts against the
Lord who stands at those doors and knocks and entreats you to let Him in and give Him room there. I
think that grief should now arise against those base,
filthy lusts which have gotten into God's room.
Desire should step forth and invite the Lord in to
take possession of that place which is His due.

I think now your hearts should begin to open

unto God, and the everlasting gates of them should
be lifted up that this King of glory might be entertained, exalted, and enthroned within you. I think
hatred should now arise in your hearts against sin,
and a contempt of the world with all the vanities
thereof. A fire of love should now begin to kindle
within you.

Look, young men, look upward. Do you see nothing? Take up the glass of the Word, and through
this perspective can you not see the Lord of heaven,
full of marvelous and most ravishing beauty in His
face? Full of most free, tender, incomparable and
incomprehensible love in His heart? If you can see
but little, beg the eye of faith and the light of the
Spirit, and then you will see wonders of beauty and
love. And do your hearts not yet begin to move towards God?

What do you say, young men? How many of your
hearts may I gain for God this day? I think every one
of you should be ready to say, "Here's my heart for
the Lord"; and "Here's *my* heart for the Lord"; and
"Here's *my* heart for the Lord." Will you now, all of
you, engage your hearts in covenant to the Lord?
Will you now withdraw your hearts from the world,
and all its lusts which have usurped them, and, making choice of God as your chief Good, devote your
hearts, with your whole man, to Him, to be His and
His forever? Consent heartily unto this, young men,
and the thing is done. Your hearts will be God's,
and God will be yours, and yours forever!

And if you would give your hearts unto God:

1. You must give them presently. Delays are dangerous; if you refuse now, you may never be asked for

them again. This may be God's last call; it may be that now you have some movings and strivings of the Spirit for your hearts; if you do not now hearken and yield, God may withhold His Spirit for the future and never strive with you again.

2. You must give them freely. Don't think that God is beholden to you to give them, but that you are beholden to Him that He will accept them.

3. You must give them fully. Don't reserve any room in them for sin, or harbor any base lust in any corner of your hearts.

4. You must give them resolutely, with full purpose never to retract this gift. God's gifts of His grace to men are without repentance; and so must be your gift of your hearts to God. And if the Lord gets your hearts this day, I know He will get all, the heart being the commanding part.

Put yourselves under God's command. Hereby you will be in safeguard from the worst of evils—I mean the reign of sin and the tyranny of the devil here, and the damnation of hell in the other world. Hereby your hearts will be near to God's heart while you live, and they shall be brought nearer to Him when you die. When absent from the body, they shall be present with the Lord in glory, and abide with Him to eternity.